Deliciously Dales

REBECCA ROBERTS & SALLY SCANTLEBURY

GREAT NORTHERN

The authors and publishers have made every effort to ensure the information contained in this book is accurate and up to date. However, they accept no liability for any loss or inconvenience caused by reliance on any material contained therein. Details of websites are for general purposes and the authors and publishers assume no responsibility for the information contained on them. If making a special journey, you are advised to phone ahead for current opening hours.

Front cover photographs
Top, left to right: The Pantry, Bolton Abbey; Hopkins & Porter Deli, Ripley; Park View Stores, Pateley Bridge; James Martin
Bottom: Beef on the hoof near Penyghent (Mike Kipling Photography)

Great Northern Books
PO Box 213, Ilkley, LS29 9WS

© Text and photographs, Rebecca Roberts and Sally Scantlebury, 2006

ISBN: 1 905080 14 X

Design and layout: Richard Joy

Printed by Quebecor Ibérica, Barcelona

British Cataloguing in Publication Data
A catalogue for this book is available from the British Library

Contents

The Dales landscape at its finest as epitomised by the view of Semerwater in Wensleydale. Take time to savour the scene before moving on to find another food champion, such as Raydale Preserves at nearby Stalling Busk. (See page 53.)

Foreword

Growing up in a catering family on the edge of the Yorkshire Dales, I was aware from a very early age of the quality and diversity of the produce available from this rich landscape.

The Yorkshire Dales is probably best known as sheep and beef farming country, and much of the produce is derived from these two activities. Dairy products feature on the shelves of independent retailers in the Dales alongside some of the best beef and lamb to be found anywhere in the country.

Farming in general has had a tough time in recent years. A sequence of events occurred over a three to four year period, each adding another hurdle to traditional farming practices which have been the lifeblood of the Dales. Foot and Mouth was probably the hardest blow with massive loss of livestock, in some cases bloodlines that had been established over many generations and will take as many again to rebuild. Through sheer determination the loss of age-old family farms was not as high as anticipated. Happily for consumers everywhere, the fields are once again stocked with cattle and sheep graze the hills and fells.

In writing this book Sally and Rebecca have met with many of these producers. Most have been touched in some way by the events of recent years. Some could not face re-stocking and have turned to farm diversification in order to provide a sustainable future for their families whilst retaining the land that is their heritage. In turn these diversified businesses provide hope for those still farming the land. A whole host of farm shops have sprung up throughout the Dales, some as part of a working farm, others in buildings that once housed cattle in the winter or provided cover for now redundant farm machinery.

It is these shops, and other independent retailers, which form the basis for six food trails around the Dales. Over a period of eight months the authors travelled the Dales and met with farmers, growers and producers to bring you the inside story behind the taste, before linking them to a wonderful selection of shops, restaurants, cafes and tea rooms which feature produce from the region on their shelves and menus.

Alongside the trails are events, farmers markets and country shows where you can meet these hardworking and dedicated custodians of the countryside. It was at one such event that I recently met up with Sally and Rebecca. Their passion for the future of farming shone through and I was delighted to be introduced to many of the producers featured within this book. The Limestone Country Beef was a joy to work with and I was particularly impressed with the baby tomatoes picked the same morning at a local organic farming co-operative.

The six trails take in some of the most spectacular scenery in Britain. Each of the dales has its own special characteristics and I hope you will enjoy exploring the area and supporting the local economy along the way. Visit the shows, support the farmers markets and enjoy some wonderful new taste experiences – beef as it used to taste, preserves prepared with fruit from the local hedgerows and cheese made with milk from cows, sheep or goats, many of which have won national awards and deservedly so.

If we are to retain the natural heritage of our countryside it is vital that we support our local farmers and food producers. The future will be tough for them. Changes in government policy is likely to be the next blow to rock these communities but with the support of our independent retailers, chefs and restaurateurs and ultimately you, the consumer, we can work together to ensure farming remains a great British tradition to be enjoyed for generations to come.

James Martin

Bill Grayson, a Dales farmer with good reason to be cheerful. He is visiting the English Nature and National Park grazing plots on Ingleborough, which are part of a project to encourage the re-growth of limestone flora through mixed grazing of cattle and sheep. The result is meat with a real flavour. (See 'Farmers from the Limestone Country project – pages 11 to 13.)

Producers with a Passion

Sunflours

Mark and Lynne Exelby took over the tenancy of the 72-hectare farm at the Hutts, near Masham, in 1986. This working farm supports 300 ewes and 35 suckler cows. By the end of the 1990s it was clear that economic prospects were not good. Diversification became the buzzword for farmers, although the options were not always obvious, and Mark and Lynne knew was no point in diversifying unless they were going to enjoy it. Thankfully everything fell in to place when a mill business in the village came up for sale.

The Exelbys decided that opening an organic flour mill-would be an ideal venture and would hopefully allow at least one of their three daughters to remain at home in the future. So they bought the entire stock of mill machinery and converted one of their stone barns at the Hutts Farm into a mill. The total cost of the project was £50,000, although help arrived in the form of a £12,000 farm diversification grant. Lynne came up with the name of Sunflours for the new business. It is bright and cheerful and has worked well, although in the first year they did get a few people wanting to order sunflowers, either seeds or plants!

Now the only commercial millers in North Yorkshire they began trading in December 2000. Mark was quite clear from the outset that they had to specialise. There was no point trying to compete with the conventional flour market, as the large commercial mills have the economy of scale and can produce flour at a lower price. The smaller business can be more flexible and develop a tailor-made product.

The core of the business is producing organic, stone ground wheat flour, which is certified by the Soil Association. Agricultural wheat is bought from a farm near Harrogate and ground in the mill, which is powered by a generator, as there is no three-phase electricity near to the farm. Many other specialised flours are also produced such as barley, maize, rye, soya and chestnut. In addition an intriguing range of blends has also been developed, some of which contain millet, poppy, sesame and – appropriately – sunflower seed.

"Our first efforts were not good," Lynne confesses, "I did a lot of bread making in order to get the mix right." She built up the business by selling the flour at farmers markets. They now have their own van covering the north of

The tiny barn converted into an empire of efficiency and attention to detail where Lynne cheerfully oversees with beauty, grace and bags of common sense.

(Left) **After a day's hard work on the farm, the couple meet in the barn to bag flour.**
(Right) **Lynne is happy to talk to customers young and old on milling techniques and bread recipes, converting to organic and contented animals. Life is never dull on the Sunflours farm.**

England and a delivery company, Moorsfresh of Pickering, distributes the flour to customers including health food stores, pizzerias, restaurants and bakeries.

There can be little doubt that Sunflours was started at the right time, as people are becoming more and more concerned about the source of their food. They realise that wholemeal flour has all the goodness left in it whilst stone grinding using ancient techniques gives an extra taste. Mark and Lynne select only the best so their flour is not cheap but it does make better bread. There has been a huge increase in the number of people using bread-making machines. They buy the flour, find it works better than the commercially produced flours and so come back for more.

The farm continues to flourish too. Spring is always a hectic time with 300 ewes to lamb but Mark has planned well to ensure the majority come along during school holidays when the children are around to lend a hand.

Sunflours flour can be found in many of our featured retail outlets, including Joneva of Masham and Park View Stores of Pateley Bridge.

Bolton Abbey Foods

The Crabtree family have farmed the land at Bolton Park Farm, in the heart of the Duke of Devonshire's estate, for three generations. Steven grew up on the farm and, along with his wife Ann, is now raising a family of his own, hoping that son Simon will keep up the tenancy in years to come.

Bolton Park is home to happy cows and sheep. A suckler herd has been established, combining the best of both native British and continental breeds. These animals are ideally suited to the lower parkland enriched by the River Wharfe which flows through the middle of the estate. The sheep are indigenous to this part of Upper Wharfedale, the flock having been established over the past forty years. Lambs are spring born and remain with their mothers right through the summer before being fattened entirely on grass thus producing sweet and succulent meat.

The farm takes in some of the most spectacular scenery in the southern Dales, starting at the famous Cavendish Pavilion, built to serve tea and cakes to the many visitors who arrived by train in the late 1800s. It continues west through the Valley of Desolation, so called because since the last Ice Age erosion by water flowing down Posforth Gill has caused the waterfall to retreat gradually from the riverbank, leaving a steep sided valley below the fall. To the east the farm encompasses much of the estate grouse moors, from which game is provided for the Devonshire Arms Hotel and Devonshire Fell at Burnsall.

Whilst Steven retains many age-old traditions in his operation of the farm, he is also an astute businessman and one of a growing number of Dales farmers who have embraced recent, often enforced, changes with a wonderful energy. Often a visit to Steven leaves us feeling exhaust-

Modern day farmer Steven Crabtree on his preferred mode of transport for getting up and down dale tending to flock and fold.

ed; he has so many ideas to ensure the farm remains a viable option for future generations of the Crabtree family.

Luckily for those who enjoy good food, many of these ideas have become reality. Not content with sending all his livestock to market and waving goodbye at the farm gate, Steven has teamed up with a local catering butcher to provide beef and lamb to some of the best dining pubs in the region. You will find beef from Bolton Abbey on the menu

at the Wellington in Darley and lamb at the award-winning Angel Inn, respectively mentioned in our Nidderdale and Wharfedale Trails. Steven thoroughly enjoys his forays into the high-powered world of beef sales, and he knows that the chefs appreciate the background knowledge that comes along with every cut of meat supplied.

Prior to taking on a new catering customer the chef is encouraged to visit the farm. Steven will take him on a tour of the fields, introduce the stock and explain how they are raised, what they have been fed on and where they will go when they finally depart from the farm en-route to the table. After this a visit is arranged with the butcher to enable the chef to discuss his preferred cuts – a truly bespoke service and one that is likely to grow in popularity in the future.

Weekends are often spent at one of the farmers markets in the area. Steven has a regular space at Grassington, Skipton and Settle markets and is keen to see this area of his trade develop. Once again his innovative mind is working to add value to an already perfect product. Alongside traditional roasts, Steven offers a selection of beef and lamb to suit almost every possible occasion. In the summer, chops are marinated ready for the barbecue and the stall will have a wonderful choice of sausages and burgers too. During the winter months these are replaced with beef for casseroles, braising and pie making.

In the summer Steven can be found in the local produce marquee at Gargrave, Malham and Kilnsey shows. This is his opportunity to meet up with customers who have supported him throughout the year and to gain valuable feedback to enable him to continue to provide some of the best quality meat in the Dales. It was at such an event that Steven met Julie Marley. She had just completed a course

at the world famous Ballymaloe cookery school, where proprietor Darina Allen believes that 'the best food comes from using the best ingredients'. Julie certainly took this on board during her time in Ireland – in fact she couldn't wait to get back to her farmhouse in Long Preston to rediscover the wonderful diversity of producers on her doorstep. Since their first meeting Julie has designed a range of recipes to the make best use of a variety of cuts. Her 'big and beefy' pies are fast gaining a reputation among local 'foodies' and she introduces an international flavour with a series of chilli dishes named after the number of people they serve.

If your visit to the area does not coincide with one of the farmers markets you can buy Bolton Abbey estate beef and lamb from The Pantry, a well-stocked store in the centre of the village. Or you can let others do the hard work and treat yourself to a meal at one of the pubs or restaurants that Steven supplies. Although the farm is not open to visitors on a regular basis, Steven and Ann welcome callers by arrangement. We usually try to make it the day before a farmers market ensuring a wide selection of fresh cuts are available.

Steven's story highlights the additional work that is created by a change in direction for many local farmers. Where once they would have spent a Monday morning chatting with friends over a coffee at the local auction market, now they could be travelling from farm shop to pub to restaurant, delivering meat or putting together a website to promote their product to discerning food buyers. We are sure they will be here for many years to come, raising happy sheep and cows and keeping local people and visitors well fed with the fine quality meat.

(Web site: www.boltonabbeyfoods.co.uk)

Farmers from the Limestone Country Project

The Limestone Country project was launched in 2002 to help preserve species of plants and flowers on over two thousand hectares of land including the Ingleborough Nature Reserve and the limestone pastures between Wharfedale and Malhamdale. It is a partnership between English Nature, the Yorkshire Dales National Park Authority and a group of fifteen of the area's farmers, who are custodians of the land in question. The project promotes mixed grazing with sheep and upland cattle that helped to create the wonderful diversity of plant species and other wildlife in the area.

Much has been written about the conservation project. There is an excellent website and regular project newsletters are available from the National Park offices in Grassington and Bainbridge. However, our story is about the farmers and their families, as without these hardworking innovators of the modern agricultural system the project would not be possible.

Sally and I were asked to help out on the project. Our brief was to create a market for the beef that would soon be made available, by the farmers in the project area, and so we went along to a meeting. What a meeting that was! Fifteen or so Dales farmers were sitting round a table in the back room at Grassington Town Hall, with a smattering of public sector officials, DEFRA and the like, thrown in for good measure. We took a deep breath and waited to be introduced.

That meeting wasn't the easiest we've ever attended – in fact it will go down in our history as possibly the toughest experience of our respective careers. Many of these farmers are used to highly commercial practices, to farming intensively and creating a super breed of beef that generates a high price in an open market. Suddenly they were being asked to forget all their previous practices and take

Wild and woolly Blue Grey cattle coming head to head on a wet and windy day. Left to graze longer than most herds and on species-rich pasture, these beasts produce excellent quality meat almost naturally infused with wild herbs.

on a collection of traditional, often rare breed, cattle that could apparently survive on some of the roughest terrain in the Dales. They took a little convincing.

We created our own Limestone Trail and in two hectic weeks visited each of the farmers on their own territory. We learned more about beef in those two weeks than many people will in a lifetime. We had lessons in the anatomy of a bullock whilst drinking tea with James Hall,

RECIPE: : Bolton Abbey Beef Wellington

Beef Wellington - Serves 6

This is a dear old favourite, which for years terrified me – how could the beef cook properly without burning the pastry? This simple-to-follow recipe worked perfectly. We used beef from Steven Crabtree at Bolton Abbey Foods and bought the pate from Kilnsey Park.

1.5 kg (3lb) fillet of beef
375g (13oz) puff pastry
225g (8oz) button mushrooms
175g (6oz) smooth liver pate
1 egg
40g (1.5oz butter)
1 tbsp vegetable oil
Pre-heat oven to 220 degrees; Gas mark 7.

Trim and tie up the beef at intervals with fine string so it retains its shape. Heat the oil and 15g (0.5oz) of the butter in a large frying pan, add the beef and seal and lightly colour on all sides. Roast for 20 minutes, allow the beef to cool then remove the string.

Fry the sliced mushrooms in the remaining butter until soft, allow to cool and mix with the pate. On a lightly floured surface, roll out the pastry into a large rectangle to a thickness of 0.5cm (quarter-inch). Spread the pate and mushroom mixture along the centre of the pastry. Place the meat on top in the centre. Brush the edges of the pastry with the beaten egg. Fold the pastry edges over and turn over so that the join is underneath, folding the ends under the meat. Place on a baking tray. Decorate with leaves cut from the pastry trimmings, brush with the remaining egg.

Bake for 50-60 minutes, covering with foil after 25 minutes. Allow to rest for 10 minutes before serving. Serve with a selection of fresh vegetables and potatoes

discussed the price of fleece with Tom Boothman whilst sitting on a bale of wool in the farmyard at Linton and played hide and seek with a herd of Blue Greys in the mist on top of Ingleborough.

Since that trip meetings have been a pleasure. We look forward to seeing the group, who have all agreed to form a marketing 'co-operative' in order to launch what promises to be a truly wonderful product into a market flooded with low quality, low cost beef.

Our enthusiasm for the product and our growing respect for the farmers has already got us in to a scrape. We recently carried out a tasting session at York Food Festival – sixty people came along and we cooked several breeds of beef to see if there was a difference in texture, cut and taste. The distinction was noticeable and this leads us to believe that soon consumers with a genuine interest in the providence of their food will be asking, not just what cut they are buying, but what breed of beef it is and from which farm it originated.

Sally has a theory that the farmers choice of traditional breed cattle reflects their own character and personality. James Hall, a well-built chap, chose the chunky Welsh Black, whilst Mrs Newhouse, who works as a nursing assistant, chose the gentle little Dexter for Newhouse Farm, the National Trust reserve on the top of Malham Moor.

Robert Phillip, with his red hair and bushy beard, chose the Highland – and this is where our problems occurred. Having recounted Sally's theory to the assembled tasters at the festival, we received a hearty laugh from our audience. As we cleared the room afterwards I found one of Robert's business cards on a table and I thought it must have slipped out of the packs that we handed out. However, a week later I was telling Robert that we had carried out a tasting session recently at York Food Festival, to which he replied, "I know, my daughter was in the audience!" Thankfully he did see the funny side, although we still cringe every time we think back to the moment when the poor girl heard her father likened to a Highland cow!

So, if you are driving on the Ribblesdale Trail, between

(Above) 'Spot the Breed' – a new family game. Whilst driving through the stunning Limestone Country landscape have fun spotting the different breeds of native cattle.

(Left) Look before you cook! The meat is darker in colour and richer in taste with creamy succulent fat, which bastes the meat making it tender and mouthwatering. The smell of this beef cooking is reminiscent of our (we were lucky!) childhood family Sunday lunches. The taste is simply sublime – a total sensory experience.

Settle and Gargrave, look out for Robert, or his Highlands. In fact, why not stop off at the farm and buy a box of the wonderful beef.

Within the project some farmers, such as group chairman Jim Caygill of Manor House Farm at Rylstone, have chosen to breed cattle. Others in the scheme can then buy from their neighbours and complete the process. Our role is to help them to select the most appropriate market for their product. We are working with chefs who are keen to feature the beef on their menus, and with butchers, such as Colin Robinson in Grassington. Some of the farmers, including Bill and Janet Whittaker who farm land on Ingleborough and Richard and Sarah Paul of Arncliffe, prefer to sell direct to the public via a box scheme. This is an ideal way to fill up the freezer for winter and get the feel-good factor that you are not only helping to sustain British farming but are also helping this most important of landscapes to thrive for future generations to enjoy.

13

Folly Ales

When travelling in the Grassington area you may come across a 'mini' bus with the slogan 'Drinking is Folly' emblazoned across the front and even, at times, scrolling along the destination panel. This has confused many a visitor to the area. When we went to the Wharfedale Brewery we heard a wonderful story about a gentleman in a nearby town who had been out celebrating one afternoon. Stumbling from a local hostelry he tripped and fell. As he clambered back up and went to cross the road, he encountered one of these buses and hasn't touched a drop since!

The Wharfedale Brewery sprung up in the garden of one of its founders, and it encountered a few problems along the way. Steve Blizzard, an American banker, re-located to the Dales and met up with David Aynesworth, a local estate manager. They shared a love of real ale and so decided to try their hand at brewing; their first 'brewery' was a folly in the garden of Steve's home. The ale was soon being enjoyed by their family and friends, and when the local paper printed a story about the two of them this was followed by a 'raid' from Customs and Excise who thought they were running a pub from their own back yard.

This incident forced a re-think – their hobby had run away with them and Folly Ale was in demand. Right from the start the objective had been to use the best ingredients and what better than natural Yorkshire water. The problem was obtaining land where a borehole could be created but in the summer of 2003 the brewery found its present home, a redundant barn at Rylstone, a short walk from the renowned Angel Inn at Hetton.

Steve and David created a brewery to handcraft a range of real ales and then employed a full-time head brewer, who had previously worked for some of the brewing giants and brought a wealth of experience to add to the passion of the founders. Adam Witek has experience gained over many years in the brewing industry, and enjoys sourcing and trying out old recipes, sometimes adding his own secret ingredients to enhance the brew. Whatever they are doing it is working! Folly Ale was the winner of the Keighley and Craven Beer Festival – the first competition the team have entered – taking first place in a selection of some 140 regional and national beers.

The award-winning Folly Ale is traditional, full-bodied Yorkshire Bitter with a distinctive lightly citrus aroma from the Goldings hops, which is followed by a rich, smooth, malty flavour and fresh after-bitterness. Executioner is the Premier Bitter, brewed to an original 1950s recipe, using pale, crystal and amber malts. This gives it a distinctive rich mahogany colour and a smooth but complex roasted malt flavour, with just the right amount of hop. Completing the regular line up is Folly Gold Smooth, a refreshing straw-coloured ale that has wonderful citrus overtones.

In terms of expansion there are no grand plans, although a steady rise in production will be needed as the word spreads. Folly is available as far afield as Kent and has even been exported to ex-pats in New Zealand, but for those wishing to enjoy the selection closer to home we rec-

Line 'em up lads! Folly Ales sits happily alongside other great independent breweries, bringing us a quality product of distinction. Don't forget 'Drinking is Folly'.

ommend a visit to one of the many hostelries that have supported the brewery from the beginning.

The Wharfedale Brewery supplies over a hundred local pubs, restaurants and shops, many of which are mentioned within this guide. You can also purchase the ales from the beer tent at local shows and events, and for guests staying in the fifteenth-century Folly apartment, just off the market place in Settle, a free bottle is provided on arrival. Their small casks are perfect for a party at home.

Commitment to independent retailers remains as strong as during the launch year. This is highlighted in the fact that sales of bottled beers are virtually on a level with sales of cask, and you will find the various ales often appear in dishes at restaurants in the area. At a recent farmers market in Settle we discovered Executioner was a key ingredi-

(Left) The tools of the trade set aside in slightly macabre fashion waiting to test The Executioner, the darker beer in the range.
(Right) "It almost makes itself," reports the modest Richard Pighills, who loves his job and cares for the vats of bubbling froth with paternal attention.

ent of a wonderful 'porter loaf' produced nearby in Cracoe.

At present the brewery is not open as a visitor centre, but it is keen to welcome small groups for a pre-booked tour and the team have various suggestions for how best to arrive. They provide route maps across some of the most scenic landscapes in the Dales and arrange for a bus to return groups to their original destination.

Cottage Cakes of Cracoe

Steve and Julia Oxby live in the pretty Wharfedale village of Cracoe, made famous as the real home of the Calendar Girls. Julia is a member of Rylstone WI, and although she decided not to participate in the calendar she is very supportive of the ladies who did and proud to be part of such a forward-going branch of the WI.

Prior to launching Cottage Cakes, Steve enjoyed a fast-moving career in marketing, whilst Julia was kept busy bringing up the children and cooking cakes for her family and friends, using the Aga in their kitchen. As their home is on the path that leads to a wonderful walk up Cracoe Fell, the family were always conscious of the number of people passing their door. As the children grew Julia took a part-time job as one of the registrars at Skipton registry office. She thoroughly enjoyed her work officiating at marriages in the district, particularly as this was around the time that many local venues were becoming licensed for wedding ceremonies.

As can be imagined this work was heavily biased towards the weekend. During the week Julia was able to indulge her love of cooking, starting to experiment more with organic ingredients for the cakes and puddings that were her forte.

Eventually the family decided to try selling some of these cakes to walkers passing the house. They went so well, and Julia was able to produce enough to sustain even the busiest of days, that Steve decided to try out a local farmers market. Northern Dales Farmers Markets had just begun in Settle when Steve first approached Alastair Davy. Having ascertained that the majority of the ingredients were locally sourced, and better still organic, Alastair agreed that the newly named 'Cottage Cakes' could come along to the next market in Settle.

Julia got to work and produced an initial range of cakes and puds, including Yorkshire Fat Rascals, the size of which we always marvel at, along with the now famous Porter Cake. This is made to a secret recipe with the addition of Executioner, the ale brewed a stone's throw away at the Wharfedale Brewery.

Their first market was a huge success and they now do at least two markets every weekend. They have spread the net further and, as well as Settle, Skipton and Grassington, they are to be found at Ashton under Lyne and Leeds too.

In accordance with the farmers market standards, ingredients are sourced locally. Free range organic eggs come from Clapham and many of the cakes and puddings are prepared and sold in line with the seasons, particularly fruit pies and crumbles. Recipes are developed from old favourites passed down through generations, many from within their own families, some handed over by interested

RECIPE: Yorkshire Fat Rascals

Although we will never make these as well as Cottage Cakes, there are occasions – in between farmers markets – when we just fancy a Fat Rascal. They are relatively quick and simple to make and we live in hope that one day we will produce them to the standard of Julia Oxby!

225g (8oz) plain flour
28g (1oz) light brown soft sugar
pinch of salt
3 tablespoons milk
110g (4oz) butter
caster sugar
55g (2oz) currants
28g (1oz) candied peel

Pre-heat oven to 180 degrees/Gas mark 5

Sift flour and salt, rub in the butter. Add the currants and sugar. Stir in the milk and about a tablespoon of water. Mix to a firm dough. Knead lightly and roll to half an inch thickness. Cut into two-inch rounds. Place on a greased baking tray. Sprinkle tops with caster sugar. Decorate with candied peel prior to baking.

Bake for about 20 minutes.

customers, and others carefully researched from old cookery books.

The range too has expanded. The 'extremely chocolaty' chocolate pudding is a chocoholic's dream, whilst the sticky toffee pudding is pure indulgence. Fruit features in the puddings with the Apple and Cinnamon Crumble Cake and the Dorset Apple Cake. Recently the business outgrew the domestic kitchen and the craft room, outside in the garden, was turned into a kitchen, which works to full capacity during the week to prepare for the weekend markets.

Steve has taken responsibility for sales and co-ordinates the various markets. They also attend as many local shows as possible, including the Leyburn Festival of Food and Autumn Feast. In 2005 they went for the first time to the York Festival of Food and Drink, which takes place during the last two weeks in September and coincides with British Food Fortnight.

(Left) Julia with her best friends at work. The prized mixer arrived to relieve some of the elbow grease, but it is still labour intensive as she hand-weighs each cake – and this woman makes a lot of cakes!
(Right) The heady aroma of freshly-baked cakes creeps up on you whilst walking up the garden path to the kitchen, where Julia can be found taking out the latest batch for cooling.

Cottage Cakes now supplies cakes and puddings to a number of local catering establishments, including Poppies tea room in Settle. Steve hopes to continue to develop this area of the business as it allows for a wider audience to sample the produce. Many who have tasted the cakes this way then become customers on the farmers market.

Growing with Grace

You can't fail to notice Growing with Grace, situated on the A65 just outside Austwick. The signs on the side of the road feature carrot 'countdown' markers and the carrot windsocks are rarely still on this rather exposed area, which to one side has far reaching-views over the to the Forest of Bowland and to the other is almost in the shadow of the Three Peaks.

Growing with Grace is an organic vegetable plantation. Started in 1999 by a group of three people, it has grown to provide employment for eighteen, each being a member of the co-operative. The organisation is certified by the Soil Association and works in harmony with the Yorkshire Organic Centre based nearby in Skipton.

An overwhelming aura of calm surrounds the site. Each task in the daily schedule of planting, nurturing and harvesting, not to mention packing and selling, is carried out in a caring environment of mutual respect. The directors and members of Growing with Grace are sympathetic to the Quaker faith and practice. They believe in four core principles – sustainable agriculture, equitable employment, workplace spirituality and fair trade.

The small, well stocked shop sells a variety of imported goods and is a major stockist of Suma products. Suma is the UK's largest independent wholesaler and distributor of quality vegetarian, fairly traded, organic and natural foods with goods ranging from toiletries to whole foods, all with the fair-trade ethics.

There are no 'bosses' here – everyone is equal. Neil Marshall, who was one of the founders of the organisation, along with his wife Debby, was brought up in Africa. His family moved back to Britain and Neil attended Harper Adams Agricultural College before returning to Kenya where he was introduced to organic agriculture.

Growing with Grace is constantly evolving. It recently became the hub for a local composting scheme, waste being collected from households in the Craven area, via the 'big pink wagon' and brought to the site. Over six thousand brown bins are provided for the collection of green household waste in north Craven. The contents are taken to the site and over sixteen weeks are turned into compost, utilising a fascinating, custom-built turning machine, before being used to increase soil fertility in the greenhouses. Even though what is brought to the site may not be organic, once the process is complete the compost can be used within the organic scheme.

Owing to the high altitude and exposed position, grow-

RECIPE: Winter Vegetable Layer Pie

Serves 4. We 'stole' this recipe from the wonderful website of the Women's Food and Farming Union. It states: 'Commonly known as half of everything, it looks beautiful with different coloured veggies. Lovely as a main dish served with wholemeal bread and salad or as an accompaniment to meat and fish dishes.' For ingredients we shopped at Settle farmers market, where the majority of the vegetables came from Growing with Grace.

1/2lb (225g) celeriac
1/2lb carrots
1/2lb swede
1/2lb parsnip
1/2pt milk
1/2pt cream
1/2pt natural yoghurt
6oz (170g) Swaledale cheese, grated
1 tsp whole grain mustard
salt and pepper

Peel all the vegetables and finely grate them in a food processor, keeping the individual vegetables separate. Layer the vegetables in an ovenproof dish, pour over the milk and cover with foil. Place in a moderate oven (180 degrees/Gas mark 5) for about 30 minutes until the veggies are cooked. Mix the cream, yoghurt, mustard, salt and pepper. When the vegetables are ready, pour this mixture over evenly and top with cheese. Return to the oven until the cheese is nicely browned (about 30 minutes on the top shelf).

ing takes place in a series of greenhouses. Alongside the rows of salad leaves and onions we came across a patch of wheat, planted by children from the local school. There is actually an underpass linking the site to the school, the children visiting regularly to tend to their crop. When the wheat matures they will go through the process of milling it into flour and baking their own bread.

In another part of the site we found a wetland area, and outside what looked like a pile of old railway sleepers was actually a wildlife habitat.

Any products that can't be grown here are sourced from fair-trade importers or other local growers. These combine to make up the popular fruit and vegetable boxes sold through the network of village post offices and shops. Orders are placed and delivered weekly and they cover an area ranging from the Craven Dales, North Lancashire, up to Kirkby Lonsdale and over to Blackburn and East Lancashire.

The salad leaves from Growing with Grace are featured on many a menu, from a soup kitchen in Accrington through to the Traddock at Austwick. Supplies to local

(Left) An unexpected flash of vibrant colour – hot chillies drying in the sun and warmth of the glasshouses. Whoever thinks it's all beef and brassicas up north needs to take a trip to our innovative growers like Growing with Grace.
(Right) Neil Marshall and his team know that growing organically is about getting the soil right. Composting and harnessing natural nutrients produce healthier crops and better food for all.

schools are growing, providing an 'apple a day' to children at Clapham village school and vegetable boxes to others that opted out of local authority contracts last year.

Produce from Growing with Grace can be found on the Grassington and Settle farmers markets and the team attend some local shows and events. The shop is open 10.00am to 5.00pm Tuesday to Saturday and visitors are welcome. Do allow some time as often the salad leaves are picked whilst you wait, guaranteeing the freshest possible produce.

Adrian Proctor – Far Cappelside

Adrian Proctor is the third generation of his family to farm the 270 acres of lowland that is Far Cappelside. To say a visit to Adrian is like stepping back in time would be to do him a great injustice; this is a combination of all that was great about farming, with a super modern twist!

We visited Adrian the day after Valentine's Day. The previous evening a friend had cooked a rack of lamb bought from Far Cappelside that weekend. This well-travelled farmer's daughter was moved to tears by the superb taste and quality of the joint in question and, having spent the morning with Adrian Proctor, it is quite obvious why.

Like so very many farms in the area, Far Cappelside was devastated by the Foot and Mouth tragedy of 2001. However, Adrian is quick to say he doesn't dwell on the past. This statement is all the more remarkable when he goes on to tell us that his farm was less than a month away from receiving full organic accreditation when his entire flock and herd were culled.

Adrian re-stocked but chose not to replace his dairy herd, opting instead for traditional breed cattle, such as

Aberdeen Angus, Shorthorn and North Devon, along with Lleyn cross Poll Dorset lambs. Soon afterwards, Far Cappelside achieved its full organic accreditation and has never looked back. Here is a farmer who is totally committed to the whole ethos of organic, the on-site cutting room ensuring a reduction in 'food miles' and offering unique flexibility in the type of cuts that are available.

Adrian appreciates that farming has changed beyond recognition, just in the years since he took over from his father. To have continued in the same vein would have involved mass expansion, just to stand still, and that was not a situation that was acceptable to him.

In order to promote his new business Adrian realised he would have to do more than simply box up a selection of joints and put an add in the local paper. He actively sought innovative marketing opportunities that he tried out on family and friends first. It was during one such session that he came across the idea of a spit roast machine that could be taken along to local shows and events. This has proved to be very popular with bookings in place for all manner of occasions, from the launch of a new piece of farm machinery through to a local society wedding. The idea was launched at the Skipton Produce Festival in 2004, slices of hot roast lamb being enclosed in a pita bread pocket and smothered in a secret sauce – it was a sell out!

Realising that traceability is becoming vital to the food buying public Adrian now cuts all his own meat and sells organic beef and lamb direct to customers and to local restaurants and pubs. Currently the Austwick Traddock

Mother and child graze peacefully together on the organic land at Far Cappelside. There is a calmness to Adrian's farm that permeates from the land to the living, with children and adults alike feeling an enhanced quality of life – thanks to all who work there.

serves Far Cappelside beef and lamb and Adrian is hoping to expand this side of the business to work with other local outlets.

When pressed to explain why Far Cappelside lamb tastes so superb, Adrian modestly stated that it must be because less intensive farming practices result in happier livestock and because of the clover-rich pasture on which they are reared.

Far Cappelside is situated in between Rathmell and Wigglesworth. Rathmell is also home to the Northern Equine Therapy Centre, otherwise known as the Horses Health Farm, a unique farm diversification established in 1991. It includes the hydrotherapy pool and solarium, and an all-weather arena for schooling and demonstrations, as well as on-site veterinary facilities, complete with an operating theatre, and a farriers' forge. The Equine Therapy Centre is open to the public at certain times of the year – it is advisable to call first to check for timings.

Although Far Cappelside farm is not open to the public

(Left) Wellingtons poised on the doorstep, ready to be sprung into at a moment's notice!
(Right) The computer sits snugly next to the Aga in Adrian's kitchen. This is where it all goes on away from the outside, cosy and comfortable yet matter of fact and functional.

on a daily basis, Adrian welcomes potential customers to view the farm and see for themselves how happy animals make for better tasting meat. If you have arranged to call on Adrian or visit the Equine Therapy Centre, you may wish to combine your trip with a visit to the Coniston Hotel, further down the A65 towards Skipton, or to Settle with its ancient market place in the shadow of Castlebergh hill. When travelling north along the A65 you will soon come to the turning for Austwick, home of the Traddock Hotel, and a little further along is Clapham and Growing with Grace – a truly organic experience.

The Blue Pig Company

For five generations the Bradley family have farmed at Merebeck a rambling farmhouse and associated buildings perched on the hillside just outside Settle. Jane Bradley is resident in the farmhouse, whilst two of her sons, Anthony and Andrew, live close by.

Their story is typical of many farming families today. In the years before Foot and Mouth they milked a hundred cows and had three hundred sheep. However, it wasn't the dreaded disease that ended this side of the business but rising costs and falling milk prices. Jane was keen for the 'lads' to seek alternative careers, and well they might have. Both the boys went off to university and gained very respectable degrees in agriculture and biochemistry, but they were determined to stay true to their roots and they set up a dry stone walling contracting business, just before Foot and Mouth struck.

Even without stock the outbreak threatened their livelihood, as they were unable to travel from farm to farm for fear of spreading the disease. The loss of their father in the same year was a blow to them all and probably the closest they have come to taking heed of their mother's words. Happily for pork lovers in the Dales they chose to stick with it thanks to some little blue pigs.

On a walling job one day the farmer offered them four piglets. Anthony was very dubious, but was keen to see stock on the farm again so he put them in the back of his van and took them home. This was in the summer of 2004 and today Gloucester Old Spot pigs are fully established on the farm.

The brothers realised from the outset that they would have to find new and different markets for the pork. They were aware of the farmers market which takes place in Settle on the second Sunday of each month so they approached Alastair Davy, who operates this and other local farmers markets to book a stall.

They now operate on three local markets, Skipton on the first Sunday in the month, Settle on the second and Ripon on the third. Their stall is one of the most attractive on the market, with its blue gingham cloth, chiller cabinet and lots of pigs adorning the space around the edges. The sales side of the business is operated by Andrew's partner Gill, who in turn is assisted by her mother. This is a family business in the true sense of the word.

RECIPE: Pork Scallop with Herby Noodles

Serves 4. This quick and easy supper dish tastes divine and takes under thirty minutes from start to finish. We used pork from the Blue Pig Company, bought from Settle Farmers Market.

500g (1lb) pork tenderloin, trimmed and cut diagonally into 10 pieces
5 tablespoons unsalted butter
170g (6oz) dried medium egg noodles
2 tablespoons chopped fresh chives
2 tablespoons chopped fresh tarragon
1/4 pint dry Martini
1 pint Chicken stock
2 tablespoons drained capers, coarsely chopped

Gently pound each piece of pork between two sheets of cling film to quarter-inch thickness with flat side of a meat pounder or a rolling pin. Pat dry and season with salt and pepper.

Heat one-and-a-half tablespoons butter in a medium-sized heavy frying pan over moderately high heat until foam subsides. Then, sauté half of pork, turning over once, until golden brown, about three minutes total. Transfer to a plate and keep warm and covered. Sauté remaining pork with one-and-a-half tablespoons butter in same manner. Reserve the pan with fat.

While meat is sautéing, cook noodles in a large pan of boiling salted water until just tender, then drain in a colander. Return to pot and toss with remaining two tablespoons butter, herbs, and salt and pepper to taste. Add Martini and capers to frying pan and deglaze by boiling, scraping up brown bits. Continue to boil until sauce is slightly thickened, about one minute.

Divide noodles among four plates and top with pork. Spoon sauce over pork.

Gill has developed the retail business, attending the markets and a variety of local food festivals throughout the year. The products, which include pork joints, bacon and gammon, have gained quite a following in the area, visitors to the stall being particularly taken with the sausages made to a recipe that Andrew helped to develop. It must be said that Anthony is a real 'foodie', often taking on the cooking at home. He is a fan of Henrietta Green and her books – 'Food Lovers' Britain' and the 'Farmers Market Cook Book'.

Our meeting was cut short by the loud crowing of a cockerel. Was this new diversification from beef and sheep farming? No – it was the ring tone on Anthony's mobile phone! His next meeting was with the National Park, with whom they are working on a planting scheme, aiming to

(Left) Good healthy piglets who even in large pens still snuggle together. Traditionally sheep and beef farmers, the Bradley brothers enjoy discovering the delights of their new livestock.
(Right) The usually smiling Anthony gets serious about farming, the changes he has experienced and his determination and enthusiasm to make it work.

plant 40,000 trees on rough grazing land around the North Craven Fault. When he's not breeding pigs, walling or working on conservation projects, Anthony is secretary of the local cricket club whilst Andrew plays rugby for North Ribblesdale..
(Website: www.thebluepigcompany.co.uk)

Rosebud Preserves

Elspeth Biltoft moved to Healey, near Masham, from the North East, in 1989. A trained dress designer, she previously made bespoke curtains. However, with a husband in the merchant navy and a young family to care for, she chose to make a living out of a hobby and launched

Elspeth Biltoft, a true food heroine. Her passion and perseverance shine through in her constant dedication to produce a perfect product. She keeps a watchful eye and practical hand in all areas of the business.

Rosebud Preserves. With help from the Rural Development Commission and a loan from Barclays bank, Elspeth was able to take eight of her favourite recipes and turn them in to a viable product base.

Rosebud Farm is just as pretty as it sounds. Set high on a hillside with spectacular views of the Wensleydale countryside, it is easy to see why Elspeth was so inspired by the wonderful variety of produce available right on her doorstep.

The Dales has many very good preserve makers, and we know they source local ingredients where possible. Elspeth is a shining example of how it should be done. A team of local people gather at Rosebud Farm for regular 'picking' trips, taking to the hedgerows to collect baskets of wild rowanberries and crab apples. Earlier in the year the same team will have been selecting elderflowers, which go into the wonderfully aromatic gooseberry and elderflower jam. Rhubarb comes from Wakefield, well known as the 'Rhubarb Capital of the North' and herbs are from nearby Sandhutton. Where it is just not possible to source locally, in the case of say Seville oranges, this does not deter Elspeth in her quest for the finest 'local' ingredients. She makes frequent trips abroad and has bought oranges from the same, family-run, grove from the outset.

In addition to the quintessentially British preserves, such as the wild crab apple and rowan, Rosebud also has a range made to authentic Indian and Malaysian recipes. These spicy and often 'hot' preserves are laced with chilli, ginger and garlic and make a perfect accompaniment to cold meats and cheeses.

Although the business continues to expand, recently converting the loft of one of the nineteenth century barns into a labelling and packing space, the products are still prepared in small batches, by hand and without the addition of preservatives or colouring. Whilst visiting we saw the team preparing cucumbers for the sweet cucumber pickle

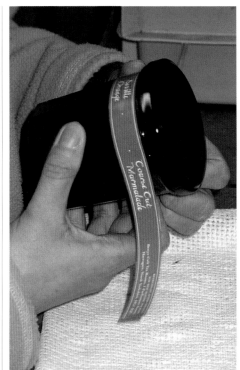

and cooking that day was a batch of their wonderful old Yorkshire chutney, without which no pork pie is complete.

Rosebud Preserves are to be found in some of the finest deli's and farm shops in the Dales. With their distinctive labels you will learn to keep an eye out for them and hope that your favourite is in season. Last autumn I became hooked on the beetroot and horseradish relish, which incidentally was a taste oasis in my, then, no fat diet. How disappointed I was to find this is only available at certain times of the year – it did spur me on to try others and now I have a favourite for every season.

If you don't see your favourite on the shelves of many of our featured retailers Elspeth is happy to mail out or advise your nearest stockist.

(Left) The care taken and attention paid to every part of the process, even putting labels on jars, is exquisite. When you taste these preserves you know you are eating something really special and this is one of the many reasons why.

(Right) Starting from scratch means you care about the product from primary produce to pot. Peeling pounds of onions may not be many people's idea of fun but at Rosebud Preserves they certainly make the most of it.

(Rosebud Preserves, Rosebud Farm, Healey, Masham, HG4 4LH. T: 01765 689174)

Swaledale Cheese

The Swaledale Cheese Company came in to being on February 16th 1986. Cheese had been made in Swaledale for many, many centuries before then, popular belief being that Cistercian monks who had travelled from Normandy first produced it in the local abbeys as far back as the eleventh century. It was originally made with sheep or goats' milk and it wasn't until the seventeenth century that the cows' milk cheese was produced in the dale. The traditional skill of cheese making was passed on to the local farmers who have handed the recipe down the generations by word of mouth.

In 1986, two days after Mandy had given birth to their daughter Louise, David Reed was made redundant. With a new baby, a mortgage and both of them out of work the future seemed uncertain. A friend suggested they tried making Swaledale cheese, which at that time it was not being produced commercially. In fact one of the last remaining producers, Marjorie Longstaff of Harkerside, was ready to retire and was keen to hand on her recipes to people with a passion. The Reeds certainly had that and after a few lessons in Marjorie's kitchen they started production at home using a ten-gallon bucket and lots of trial and error.

Mandy remembers those visits to the Longstaffs with great fondness. They kept a cow and a pig, which fed them through the winter months, and the power was run by a generator that was turned on each evening for the nine o'clock news. When Mr Longstaff died, Marjorie moved down from Harkerside in to Reeth, where she maintained her lifelong ties with the dale and knitted socks for Swaledale Woollens.

Luckily David and Mandy had the right credentials to launch the business. David had been a chef and Mandy had worked in food sales – although it wasn't easy with a new baby and a new business. Initially Mandy contacted the large distributors, who at first were not interested in a new cheese. David and Mandy made small batches, around fifteen cheeses a week; imagine their delight when Anthony Rowcliffe, one of the largest distributors of cheese in the UK, placed an order for fifty! Mandy strapped their two week old baby into the van and drove to London and back in a day to deliver their first order personally. Nothing happened for three weeks but then came the next order, this time for a hundred.

They were off – and the business soon outgrew the family kitchen. They borrowed a friend's business unit but at the suggestion of their friendly Environmental Health Officer they quickly moved to their own purpose-built premises. This is where they remain today, although several additions have been made to the unit and they are currently expanding again.

Originally David and Mandy made cheese with cows'

Caring and sharing the workload, Mandy and the lads have a laugh before getting 'hands on' into the curds and whey.

milk. Historically the recipe would have used sheep's milk, but the tradition lapsed as fewer people milked sheep, considering it a slightly strange practice. Happily the tradition was revived and the Swaledale range now includes a cows' milk, a sheep's milk and a goats' milk cheese. I was intrigued to know how these are kept separate in production, particularly as my husband can spot goats' cheese at a hundred paces and backs away quickly! Mandy explained that they have a 'cow day', a 'sheep day' and a 'goat day', and each has its own maturing room. The recipes remain true to the original passed on by Mrs

(Left) There is a good mould and a bad mould on cheese but no bad mould here. These individuals are perfectly well behaved, waiting in line to be picked and packed and sent to their new home, there to be devoured by a delighted customer.
(Right) Each cheese is delicately handled and lovingly brushed to create the perfect natural rind. This is done regularly as they progress from 'being our babies' to full maturity.

Longstaff, each being adapted to suit the particular milk **27** used. Over the years additions have been made, two of the cheeses now going off to Mackenzies Smokehouse, featured on our Nidderdale Trail. Traditional Swaledale is gently smoked with oak chippings and then matured for three weeks. This results in a perfect balance between the moist texture of Swaledale and the mellow oak smoking, giving it a subtle nutty flavour. Swaledale Goats' Cheese is gently smoked over oak chippings for two days, the result being a creamy moist cheese with a mild smoked flavour and a rich velvety texture. Another is enhanced by the addition of four fluid ounces of Theakston Old Peculier to every pound of curd. The finished cheese has a marbled appearance, a soft texture and leaves you in no doubt of its Old Peculier flavour.

Two of the cheeses are infused with fresh herbs. The Swaledale cheese is hand-made with full fat cows' milk to the traditional farmhouse recipe and then, before pressing, freshly chopped basil and the best Italian sun-dried tomatoes are gently mixed into the curd. The combination of the creamy moist Swaledale and Mediterranean flavours

results in a truly memorable cheese, excellent for cooking in salads or just on a cheeseboard. The Swaledale with Chives and Garlic is just 'morish'.

The most recent addition is an organic cheese with milk coming from Hazel Brow, an organic farm and visitor centre included in our Swaledale Trail. All the milk for Swaledale Cheese is produced locally, Mandy having an arrangement with Dairy Farmers of Great Britain to ensure that it comes from local farms.

All this hard work has paid off and Swaledale Cheese is regularly to be found among the award winners at national and international competitions. To their great credit the Swaledale Cows' Milk and the Swaledale Ewes' Milk received 'Product of Designated Origin' over ten years ago, being among the first cheeses in the country to undergo this extremely lengthy process. All the paperwork has to go through Brussels and takes at least two years to complete.

This story, however, is tinged with sadness. David Reed died suddenly in July 2005, having built up the business, along with Mandy and their two children, from their domestic kitchen to supplying such prestigious stores as Selfridges and Harrods and employing a team of staff at the unit in Richmond. Mandy is determined to keep the business moving forward, and has now been joined full time by their daughter Louise, her assistant on their very first delivery. Louise is now nineteen and an active full time member of the team, and Mandy hopes that Sam will join too when he completes his studies.

We are particularly fond of the Swaledale brand as all concerned have remained so true to their roots. They regularly attend farmers markets in the area and some of their best customers remain Elijah Allen, mentioned on our Wensleydale Trail, and Muker Stores.
(Web site: www.swaledalecheese.co.uk)

RECIPE: Quick Summer Supper

4 X individual 100g goats' cheeses - or two-inch thick rounds cut from a larger piece
olive oil
fresh basil leaves
4 large plum tomatoes
freshly ground black pepper and sea salt
4 tablespoons of your favourite preserve - works well with Rowan Jelly from Rosebud or Raydale Blackberry Jelly

Place the goats' cheese in individual ovenproof dishes. Drizzle with olive oil. Season with salt and pepper. Roughly chop the basil and sprinkle over. Slice the tomato and place a couple of slices on top of the basil. Dollop on a generous tablespoon of you chosen preserve.

Bake in a hot oven (190 degrees/Gas mark 5) for about 15 minutes until the cheese is soft through but not melted.

Serve with a crisp green salad.

Allan Ellis – Rushyford Game

In the space of just two years, and thanks to the support and contacts gained from Northern Dales Farmers Markets, Allan Ellis has been catapulted into the forefront of game sales across Britain. The owner of Rushyford Game, he is Deer Management Level 2 qualified and has managed deer from Fort William through to the southern Dales.

Following a career in the Army which spanned every continent and lasted for nineteen years, Allan returned to his home town in County Durham and worked in a variety of jobs. Throughout this time he pursued his hobby and passion of game shooting. Allan's job, working nights in an engineering factory, meant his days were free; he would often shoot in the early morning before sleeping ready for the next night shift. Initially Allan sold game to larger dealers, but he decided to try selling some direct

and went to his first farmers market in Darlington.

All the game that Allan sells is wild and not farmed. He has built up relationships with many estates in the north of

(Left) Allan, with his quick turn of phrase and occasionally colourful language, tells it like it is and how it could be for you. He tells stories of how game is caught, killed, cut and cooked, bringing about a better awareness and understanding of food culture. Wild game is now included on the menus of organic and non-organic restaurants and Allan gives lectures to chefs on the versatile use of game meat and products.

(Right) There are endless possibilities for delicious dishes using these versatile tasty meats. Allan Ellis and his chef son Stuart share their passion and knowledge by demonstrating how easy and what fun it can be.

Feather and fur and the subsequent meat open up a whole world of culinary opportunity. Bought from a reputable game dealer, fresh, healthy, seasonal and traceable meat is available in such a variety of forms and flavours that it is breathtaking.

England and here he buys game from the shoots. Parties enjoy a day's shooting and get to take some of the 'bag' home, Allan buying the rest from the gamekeepers on the estate.

For a while Allan kept up the day job, or in his case the night job, taking on more and more farmers markets all the while. It was his bank manager who finally persuaded him to go full time into direct sales and he has never looked back. One farmers market turned into over twenty and through these events Allan met chefs and retailers who also wanted to source fresh, wild game. As more and more people realise the health benefits of eating game, lower in fat and with no additives or preservatives, so Allan's business has grown. He now supplies many local restaurants,

including the Angel at Hetton and the Austwick Traddock, which is the only hotel in the North of England to have a Soil Association organic certified restaurant – wild game is allowed under the rules of certification.

The farmers markets have also provided Allan with some contacts in 'high places'. When Prince Charles and the Duchess of Cornwall visited Richmond farmers market, Allan was delighted to chat about his work. The Prince offered him muntjac deer from his estate and Allan recalls, "He remembered me from when I'd met him before. He wanted to know when I was going to start supplying game to London and I told him I'd started a trial a month ago. It's going well."

Allan has a fantastic rapport with his customers. When we visited him on Grassington farmers market he was enjoying a conversation with two of his more elderly customers. It would appear that they had been 'out of circulation' during the late summer and into the hard winter, returning on a bright spring morning. Allan had not forgotten them and was cheerfully providing them with two venison burgers each, along with a couple for their friend – a new, and sure to be regular, visitor to the market. It was a real pleasure to watch Allan in action.

Recently he has moved into new areas, taking time out from the markets. With the assistance of a new partner in the business, he spends time in local colleges where he works with students in their final year to pass on his knowledge of wild game. He takes them through every step of the process so they fully understand where the game has originated, seasonality and, most importantly, preparation of the meat. Allan hopes this initiative will help to increase awareness of this most important of British ingredients and that, in years to come, game will feature more prominently on menus in a wider selection of restaurants and pubs. (Rushyford Game, 3 The Cottages, Rushyford, Ferryhill, Co Durham, DL17 0LN; web site www.rushyfordgame.co.uk)

The Nidderdale Trail

Our Nidderdale Trail starts in the tiny village of Ripley, dominated by the beautiful castle with wonderful walks. The 'park walk' takes you round the castle's large ornamental lake, across the waterfall and into the deer park. The gardens are also home to the National Hyacinth collection, best seen in April and May.

On entering Ripley you can't fail to notice the Boar's Head (1). This traditional coaching Inn is furnished from the 'attics' of Ripley Castle, courtesy of Sir Thomas and Lady Ingleby who both take an active role in the day to day running of the whole estate. There are two dining choices here, the more formal restaurant and the bistro where we highly recommend the home-baked bread served as a loaf to cut up at the table. Game from the estate is featured alongside other locally sourced produce.

In the castle courtyard there is a fabulous deli-style farm shop, Hopkins & Porter (2), where you will find products from most of our featured producers. The shop was established in 1983 by Mervyn and Catherine Moorse, who together source the best local produce to complement an international range of artisan foods, along with a huge selection of beers and wines from around the world.

On leaving Ripley follow the B6165 through the village of Burnt Yates and on to Summerbridge. A little further along the road you will enter Glasshouses and we do recommend a visit to Yorkshire Country Wines (3), established in 1989 by Richard and Gillian Brown. In the cellars of a nineteenth-century flax mill they produce a range of fruit wines, such as elderberry, blackberry and rhubarb, alongside the traditional wassail cup – a spiced elderberry and blackberry wine. This makes a superb base for mulled wine. It is hard to choose when is the best time to visit this fascinating venue. In December a warming wassail cup is served to visitors after enjoying the winery tour.

However, summer is the best time to benefit from the superb setting, starting with the approach on a tree-lined path running alongside the river Nidd. A refreshing afternoon tea served on the riverside patio is an attraction in itself, reminiscent of the south of France or Tuscany and in fact used as a location for the television series 'The Darling Buds of May' with actor David Jason.

We mustn't forget the reason for a visit. Marvel at the huge water turbine, housed twenty feet below the floor and viewed through a glass panel and join the winery tour to learn how these country wines are produced traditionally from fruits and flowers. This is done without the use of grape juice, using recipes that have been tried and tested over many years of family winemaking. The processes are

Open the shop door of Hopkins & Porter Deli from the quiet bright courtyard and discover a riot of products, local and home-made, displayed alongside national and international fine foods.

31

(Top) Enter into another world and relax in the peace and tranquillity of Yorkshire Country Wines. Even in winter this place seems green and lush and equally fascinating.

(Lower) Experience a tasting tour and take time deciding your favourite tipple. Richard and Gillian share with you the story behind their product.

not unlike those you would use at home, only on a much larger scale. Most of the fruit is brought locally from the growers, and friends of Richard and Gillian pick the elderflowers in June every year.

Next stop is Pateley Bridge. If you intend to stay overnight, Talbot House **(4)** is lovely. We enjoyed meeting proprietor Stephen Burden, who realised his dream of owning a busi-

THE NIDDERDALE TRAIL MAP KEY

❶ The Boar's Head ✆ 01423 770 152 ⓘ www.boarsheadripley.co.uk & **Ripley Castle,** Ripley ✆ 01423 770 152 ⓘ www.ripleycastle.co.uk

❷ Hopkins-Porter (Wine & Cheese) Ltd., Delicatessen, The Old Stable Shop, Ripley Castle, Harrogate, HG3 3AY ✆ 01423 771466 ⓘ www.portersripleycastle.com

❸ Yorkshire Country Wines, Riverside Cellars, The Mill, Glasshouses, Harrogate, HG3 5QH ✆ 01423 71194 ⓘ www.yorkshirecountrywines.co.uk

❹ Talbot House, 27 High Street, Pateley Bridge, Harrogate HG3 5AL ✆ 01423 711597 ⓘ www.talbothouse.co.uk

❺ The Oldest Sweet Shop in England, 39 High Street, Pateley Bridge, Harrogate, HG3 5JZ ✆ 01423 712371 ⓘ www.oldestsweetshop.co.uk

❻ T Kendall & Son, Butcher, High Street, Pateley Bridge, HG3 5JZ, ✆ 01423 711 342

❼ H. Weatherhead & Sons Butchers, 9 High Street, Pateley Bridge, HG3

5HG ✆ 01423 711 207

❽ Park View Stores, Bridge House Gate, Pateley Bridge, HG3 5HG ✆ 01423 711 923

❾ Sportsman's Arms, Wath-in-Nidderdale, Pateley Bridge, Harrogate, HG3 5PP ✆ 01423 711306 ⓘ info@signpost.co.uk www.sportsmans-arms.co.uk

❿ Yorke Arms, Ramsgill, Harrogate, HG3 5RL ✆ 01423 755 243 ⓘ www.yorke-arms.co.uk

⓫ Tea Room @ How Stean Gorge, Lofthouse, Pateley Bridge, Harrogate, HG3 5SF ✆ 01423 755666 ⓘ www.nidderdale.co.uk

⓬ The Wellington Inn, Darley, Harrogate, HG3 2QQ ✆ 01423 780362 ⓘ www.wellington-inn.co.uk

⓭ Scaife Hall Farm, Blubberhouses, Otley, LS21 2PL ✆ 01943 880 354 ⓘ www.scaifehallfarm.co.uk

⓮ Mackenzies Yorkshire Smokehouse, 1-6 Hardisty Hill, Blubberhouses, LS21 2PQ ✆ 01943 880369 ⓘ www.mackenziesyorkshiresmokehouse.co.uk

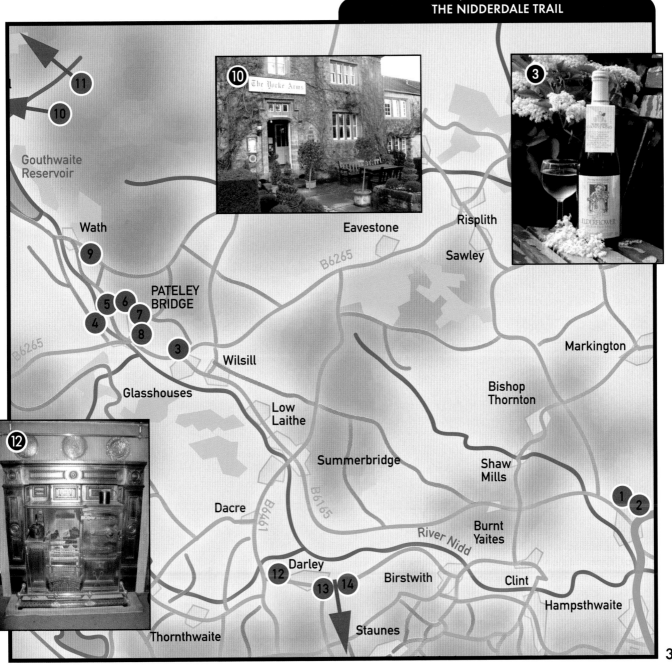

The darker dale of Nidd is home to the majestic Gouthwaite Reservoir, with its nearby picnic area, where it is worth stopping to watch the play of light on land and water.

ness in the Yorkshire Dales when he took over in 2002. Since then Stephen has introduced local produce onto the fine and hearty breakfast menus and within the substantial packed lunches. These form part of the walkers' pack along with Ordnance Survey Explorer map, guidebook describing the route, day-by-day itinerary, information on places to stop for refreshments along the way and a list of local facilities – banks, shops, post offices and the like.

For those just passing through there are plenty of great shops. Children of all ages must visit the 'Oldest Sweet Shop in England' **(5)**, a wonderful building which dates back to 1630. The business itself was established in 1827 and has been a source of delight to visitors ever since, with the shelves just groaning with old-fashioned sweetie jars. The proprietors Gloria and Keith Tordoff took over around ten years ago, due in part to Keith's sweet tooth – "it was cheaper to buy a sweet shop". They still use an original till

and Avery scale with brass dishes to weigh out sweets – although weights have moved on and the old 'quarter' of midget gems has become 113 grams!

Pateley Bridge is lucky to have two superb family butchers. T Kendall & Son **(6)** is of thirty-four years standing and is situated at the top of the High Street. All their products contain meat from the family farm and pies are made in the bake house on site. Lynne is happy to talk about the various cuts of meat and offer cooking tips to get the most from the wonderful flavours, only found in traditionally hung meats, whilst Mike prides himself on an array of sausages including Leek & Ginger, Blue Stilton & Broccoli, and the renowned Dales and gluten-free. Michelle, Lesley, Jayne, Elaine and Sarah are the team in the bake house. Their prize-winning, speciality pork pies include apple, chutney, sage & onion stuffing and cranberry.

Also on the High Street is Weatherheads Butchers, founded by Harry Weatherhead in 1876, another traditionally run family business that has passed from generation to generation. It is continued today by brothers Ian and Andrew Weatherhead, along with business partner Stephen Curtis. Andrew's wife Sally runs the family farm and they also source champion cattle, sheep and pigs to provide additional stock to complement their own. Weatherheads is the current holder of the National Small Pork Pie Championship and is frequented by the 'rich and famous' both locally and from further afield. TV personality Janet Street-Porter, in a Times article, named Weatherheads her 'favourite shop of any in the country'.

Wandering through Kings Court, a former coaching inn courtyard just off the High Street, visit the Brymor Ice Cream Shop. We feature Brymor in the Wensleydale Trail but you don't have to visit the creamery to enjoy ice cream made on the farm. Here there are over twenty delicious flavours in cones and take-home packs.

Park View Stores has been run by the Wilson family for twenty-six years, Malcolm and Dorothy along with their son and daughter making the business a real family affair. As well as selling many locally produced goods, such as

(Above) A rare quiet moment in the dining room at The Wellington, normally bustling with happy customers, locals and visitors eating and drinking together. Their fantastic blackboard menu signals the use of fresh local produce in innovative home-made dishes.

(Right) Chef Dean in the kitchen at the Wellington Inn at Darley, preparing and serving 'proper food in proper portions' sourced locally from Nidderdale and beyond.

flour from Sunflours and local cheeses from Wensleydale and Swaledale, the business incorporates a thriving bakery. It produces breads, pies, quiches and pastries – and is locally famous for its flapjack. The shop is open seven days a week and delivers to the local area.

On leaving Pateley Bridge you are faced with several choices of route. Take the B6265 to visit Brimham Rocks and continue on to Fountains Abbey, or head west on the same road to join the Wharfedale Trail at Grassington. Alternatively, continue up Nidderdale where you will come across two superb dining establishments – the Sportsman's Arms at Wath and, a little further along, the Yorke Arms at Ramsgill. The two sit at either end of

Gouthwaite Reservoir and the hardest part will be deciding which of them to visit. The Sportsman's Arms (9) has been run since 1978 by Ray and Jane Carter and family; the atmosphere is cosy and unpretentious whilst the menu features locally reared meats, game in season and a vast selection of fish delivered daily from Whitby.

Maybe more suited to a special occasion is the Michelin-starred Yorke Arms at Ramsgill, run by one of the country's best female chefs, Frances Atkins. An eighteenth century coaching house and shooting lodge, it is situated on the edge of the village green. The Yorke Arms is one of Britain's leading restaurants with rooms and its excellence has been acclaimed by the major guide publications. Locally sourced produce is in abundance and the menus

Purveyor of his shop selling products smoked on site, Robert adds other local specialist produce from the region. What some may consider occasional treats due to their superior quality, there is in fact an abundance of affordable delicacies readily available at this 'must stop' shop.

more than worthy of their high acclaim.

Nearing the end of this branch of the Trail do make time to visit the superb bird sanctuary at Gouthwaite Reservoir or travel a little further to How Stean Gorge, known for its dramatic limestone cleft that is eighty feet deep in places. If refreshments are required this is an ideal place to rest. The Restaurant and Tearoom (11), run by Antony & Eleanor Meade, is famous for serving 'Sunday Lunch' everyday. The home-cooked meals include vegetarian dishes and on a fine day you can dine on the terrace.

From this point we recommend a return to Pateley Bridge, where you can follow the signs for Summerbridge to take you to the A59 via the village of Darley. Here we were delighted to find the Wellington Inn (12), recently taken under the wing of Chris Monkman, famed for his commitment to local sourcing. Having worked his magic on the Fleece at Addingham, Chris was looking for a new challenge and happily for Darley he chose the Wellington. Menus are extensive – we love to see a blackboard as we feel it signifies an ever-changing fare – and we were not disappointed. Locally reared lamb from Colin Robinson, the Grassington butcher, is featured alongside beef from Bolton Abbey Foods.

As we come towards the end of the Trail, join the A59 and head towards Skipton. As you drop down the hill at Hopper Lane turn right and climb a short steep hill, passing on your left the farm-stay property of Scaife Hall Farm (13). It is worth calling in here to stock up your freezer with Swaledale lamb reared on the farm.

At the brow of the hill is Mackenzies Smokehouse (14). The origins of the business are fascinating, the smoking originally taking place in the cellar of an Italian restaurant in Harrogate. Frustrated at being unable to obtain high-quality smoked products, Peter Mackenzie decided to do it himself. Inevitably the business outgrew its humble roots and having moved to its present site it was taken over ten years ago by Robert and Stella Crowson. Stella trained at Westminster College as a Cordon Bleu cook and took on responsibility for sales whilst Robert was in charge of production. The business has developed from simply salmon in the early days to a point where almost anything can now be smoked on site. They also cure bacon and hams, always sourcing British meats from as close to the site as possible.

Mackenzies supply many deli's, farm shops and restaurants in the Dales and through a national delivery company have customers in the south of England too. The quality of their product could be due to the fact that they only burn pure oak, giving the best possible natural flavour to anything from a kipper to a smoked goose! Vegetarians are catered for too, with a wide variety of smoked cheeses from the Wensleydale and Swaledale creameries.

The Crowsons have recently opened their own outlet where, alongside the smoked products, they feature goods from some of the region's best-known producers. You can pick up plenty of accompaniments to complement your choice of smoked produce.

This ends the Nidderdale Trail. From here you can take the A59 towards Skipton and join the Wharfedale Trail at Bolton Abbey.

The Wharfedale Trail

The Wharfedale Trail is reached from the Wensleydale Trail via the A684 from Hawes, through the pretty village of Bainbridge and on to Aysgarth, where you may wish to spend time visiting the spectacular Falls. From Aysgarth head towards West Burton and into Bishopdale, climbing to the head of the valley at Kidstones Pass. The road descends to Cray passing the White Lion, the highest pub in Wharfedale.

Just below Cray the road branches off to Hubberholme, where the George Inn serves a great pint of Black Sheep ale, alongside many other local favourites. A little further along this road is the hamlet of Yockenthwaite with just three dwellings, but surprisingly there are now two thriving local businesses here. Yockenthwaite Farm (1) is situated on the north bank of the River Wharfe and is a working hill farm that has been in the same family for over 160 years. Stuart and Elizabeth Hird sell lamb, naturally reared, grazing on the herb rich pastures that are so special to this area of the Yorkshire Dales. Non- intensive traditional hill shepherding means the lambs are reared to the highest welfare standards, enabling them to mature slowly in the old fashioned way, producing a tender and succulent flavoursome meat. This is meat like it used to taste!

Close by is the home of David Finnell, who knows that pre-packaged flour and oats lose valuable nutrients. With his home milling system you can prepare your grains fresh in your own kitchen with mills, flakers, and UK grains, or buy fresh-milled porridge oats and Granola cereals baked here in the new Bread of Life Yockenthwaite Bakery (2).

Our Trail begins in earnest at Kettlewell, setting for the 2003 'Calendar Girls' film. If you haven't planned to take a meal break here, do at least make time to visit the Village Store (3), a 'foodie' paradise for locals and visitors alike. The Store, owned by the McClellan family, is a treasure

trove of local produce and here you will find cheeses from Ribblesdale and Wensleydale dairies, milk and cream from Grassington, *Limestone Country Beef* and a full selection of bottled beers by *Folly Ales*. The Store offers Internet access so visitors can check their emails whilst stocking up on great produce from the area.

Leaving Kettlewell, proceed down Wharfedale on the B6160 and look to your left across the sweeping valley to the River Wharfe below. On these limestone pastures you

Kettlewell Village Store is the epitome of community shopping, where local produce adorns the shelves for residents and tourists alike. There are far too few such places where you can dash in knowing you will find what you need or alternatively sit and have a chat, sample freshly baked goods, admire local artifacts, grab a gift, buy a stamp, deliberate over fine wines and even send an email.

37

may encounter cattle from the *Limestone Country Beef* project, one of our featured producers.

Kilnsey, with its spectacular limestone crag, is the next village on the trail and home to a wonderful Trout Farm and Tea Room **(4)**. Anthony and Vanessa Roberts have created a whole range of activities to suit all ages and abilities. Children will love to feed the trout which swim in clear water ponds, fed by a spring originating from the limestone hillside above, or take the Red Squirrel Trail, a recent addition to the Park and an important conservation project in its own right. The Tea Room is open daily for morning coffee, lunch and afternoon tea. As might be expected, the speciality is the trout prepared in all manner of ways, with their battered trout being a real favourite. Visitors rarely leave without checking out the deli-style farm shop where home-made ready meals and trout pates and terrines feature alongside the wonderful *Stamfrey Farm Clotted Cream*. Smoked products are from Mackenzies, mentioned in our Nidderdale Trail and cheese is from the Hawes Creamery in Wensleydale.

Our trail now moves on to Grassington, passing through

Threshfield where Wood Nook **(5)** is *THE* 'foodie' caravan park, with it superb site shop. Here Hayley Thomson has indulged her passion for local produce to bring you the fabulous clotted cream from Stamfrey farm, home-baked organic cakes by *Cottage Cakes* of Cracoe and a wonderful choice of award-winning meat and game pies from Anthony Stern of I's Pies.

Grassington is actually a small town, although the locals often refer it to as a village. The *Northern Dales Farmers Market* takes place on the third Sunday of the month in the

RECIPE: Hot Smoked Trout Pate

Serves two as a light meal or four as a starter. This recipe is so versatile you'll wish you'd had it for years. We rarely pass by Kilnsey Park without popping in for some of their delicious smoked trout, so simple yet good enough to serve at the finest of dinner parties and all in under five minutes from shopping bag to plate.

1 hot-smoked trout approximately 650g (1lb 5oz)
225g (8oz) cream cheese (1 small tub)
1 handful snipped chives
Horseradish to taste - use either creamed or grate some fresh
Single cream

Flake the fish from the bone. Place all ingredients except the cream in a blender and process until smooth, adding the cream to create the desired consistency

Best served with chunky fresh bread and a squeeze of lemon, the hot smoked trout could be replaced by one of the flavoured varieties. Garlic and dill works just as well and is particularly suited to summer picnics.

THE WHARFEDALE TRAIL MAP KEY

1 **Stuart & Elizabeth Hird,** *Yockenthwaite Farm, Buckden, Skipton, BD23 5JH* © 01756 760835 ⓘ www.yockenthwaite-farm.co.uk *Visitors by appointment only*

2 **David Finell, Bread of Life, New House Farm,** *Deepdale, Skipton, BD23 5JJ* © 01756 760811 ⓘ www.grains2mill.com *Visitors by appointment only*

3 **Kettlewell Village Store,** *Kettlewell, Skipton, BD23 5QX* © 01756 760221 ⓘ www.kettlewellvillagestore.co.uk

4 **Kilnsey Trout Farm,** *Kilnsey Park, Kilnsey, Skipton, BD23 5PS* © 01756 752150 ⓘ www.kilnseypark.co.uk

5 **Wood Nook Caravan Park,** *Skirethorns, Threshfield, Skipton, BD23 5NU* © 01756 752412 ⓘ www.woodnook.net *Bookings or visitors by appointment*

6 **The Yorkshire Lass,** *6 Main Street, Grassington, BD23 5AP*

© 01756 751 835 ⓘ www.feast-net.net

7 **Colin Robinson, Family Butcher** *41 Main Street, Grassington, Skipton, BD23 5AA* © 01756 75247

8 **Foresters Arms,** *20 Main Street, Grassington, Skipton, BD23 5AA* © 01756 752349

9 **Craven Arms,** *Appletreewick, Skipton,* © 01756 720 252

10 **The Red Lion,** *Burnsall, Skipton, BD23 6BU* © 01756 720204 ⓘ www.redlion.co.uk

11 **The Devonshire Fell Hotel,** *Burnsall, Skipton, BD23 6BT* © 01756 729000 ⓘ www.devonshirefell.co.uk

12 **The Pantry,** *Bolton Abbey, Skipton, BD23 6EX,* © 01756 715 8 000

13 **The Devonshire Arms Country House Hotel and Spa,** *Skipton, BD23 6AJ* © 01756 710441 ⓘ www.thedevonshirearms.co.uk

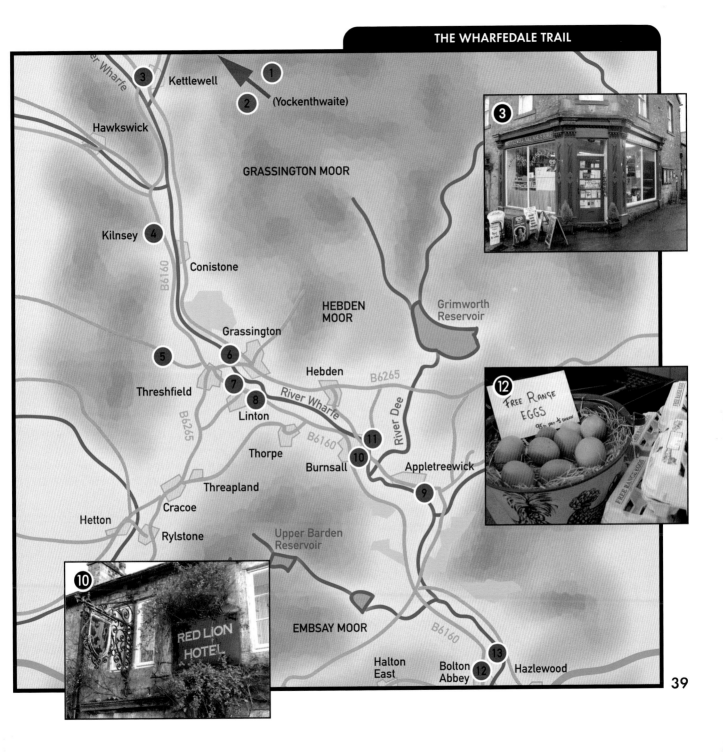

① (Yockenthwaite)

② Kettlewell

③

④ Kilnsey

⑤ Threshfield

⑥ Grassington

⑦

⑧ Linton

⑨ Appletreewick

⑩ RED LION HOTEL

⑪

⑫ FREE RANGE EGGS 95p per ½ dozen

⑬ Bolton Abbey

River Wharfe
Hawkswick
GRASSINGTON MOOR
Conistone
B6160
HEBDEN MOOR
Grimworth Reservoir
Hebden
B6265
River Wharfe
River Dee
B6265
B6160
Thorpe
Burnsall
Threapland
Cracoe
Hetton
Rylstone
Upper Barden Reservoir
EMBSAY MOOR
B6160
Halton East
Hazlewood

39

Kilnsey Trout Farm

* Local Pheasant £4.50/kg
* Wild Mallard £5.95/kg
* Wood Pigeon £2.80 each
* Wild Rabbit £4.60/kg
* Hare (when available) P.O.A

GATE OPENING TIMES:
9am - 5.30pm (Dusk in winter)

'town' centre. If you visit at any other time you can still find a wealth of locally produced goods and refreshments in the many pubs, cafes, hotels and restaurants. We highly recommend the Yorkshire Lass (6) at the entrance to the Square. Lindsay Hobbs and her team bake daily and their homemade fruitcake is truly delicious. Not content with selling from her own shop at Wood Nook, Hayley has influenced her friends in the village and Lindsay is now a Yorkshire clotted cream convert. You will receive a generous helping alongside any of the homemade puds and a scone with local jam would not be the same without lashings of clotted cream piled on top.

If you have time to browse you will be delighted by the range of shops in Grassington, mostly owner run, some by second and third generations of the same family.

Colin Robinson (7) , the butcher, is one of the few retail outlets in the Dales to stock *Limestone Country Beef.* We love the

(Left) A great place to take the family, connect with the countryside and pile inside for fantastic fresh food, Kilnsey Trout Farm provides food cooked with love and care and served by friendly staff. Tuck in to delicious simple food often produced right outside the door. When it's this good, who could resist buying some to take home?
(Right) Signs at the Trout Farm have a distinctive flavour all of their own.

element of surprise – what breed will be available today? Might it be Welsh Black from James Hall at Darnbrook Farm on Malham Moor, or Blue Grey from Bill Whittaker whose land is on Ingleborough, or possibly Shorthorn produced at Linton by farmer Tom Boothman. Our recent test sessions showed a marked difference in taste between the breeds and we are sure that in less than five years we will all be requesting beef by the breed, just as we now know which grape produced our wine or what variety of apples we prefer.

If you have time for lunch or dinner in Grassington we recommend the Foresters Arms **(8)**. Colin Robinson supplies meat here so you can be sure you are supporting two local businesses, and you may find *Limestone Country Beef* on the menu too.

From Grassington you can choose to head off to Hebden and on to join the Nidderdale trail, or continue along the Wharfedale trail. Turning left in Threshfield you can make

RECIPE: Terrine of Rabbit with Chestnuts

The Devonshire Fell Hotel and Restaurant

4 breasts of rabbit - from Allan Ellis on Skipton, Grassington or Settle Farmers Market
250g (9oz) pork mince - from the Blue Pig Company
250g (9ox) chicken liver, diced
1 egg, beaten
2 shallots, finely chopped - from Growing with Grace
A sprig of rosemary, finely chopped
1 bay leaf
Pork call - to line the tin and parcel the pâté
10cl of port wine
100g (4oz) chestnuts coarsely chopped

Ask Allan, or your chosen butcher, for the equivalent of four breasts in diced rabbit meat. Mix the rabbit with the rosemary and some salt and pepper.

Dice the chicken liver and cover in a dish with the port wine. Leave to marinate in the fridge for 20 minutes.

Mix the shallots with the rabbit, the pork mince and the egg.

Use a loaf tin or similar oven-proof dish. Cover it with pork call so it comes up the sides of the dish leaving enough to cover the top of the pate to make a parcel. Divide the rabbit mix in half and press one half of the mix well into the dish. Follow this with a layer of all the chicken liver mix and then the final amount of the rabbit mix. Top with a bay leaf and fold over the pork call to cover the terrine.

Set the oven to 190 degrees/Gas Mark 5. Fill a roasting tin with boiled water. Place the loaf tin carefully in the boiling water without covering it and put in the oven for two hours. Leave to cool, and serve in slices.

Friendly Grassington butcher Colin Robinson prides himself on specializing in the best quality meat from the local area. A warm welcome awaits customers at his shop where staff help continue a tradition of knowledgeable and amiable customer service ensuring return trade time and time again.

a short detour to visit the tiny village of Linton, where on the approach you may catch a glimpse of Tom Boothman's *Limestone Country Beef* herd grazing the fields. Look out for 'the funny little black cows'.

More choices present themselves at Linton. Either re-trace your journey for a mile or so and proceed on to Burnsall or take the B6265, joining the end of the Malhamdale trail at Cracoe.

If you choose to stay with the Wharfe your journey will

When you get a chance, pull over, get out the car or off the bicycle and stop. Breathe in the Wharfedale air, take in the view, open your heart and realise just how fortunate we really are.

follow the river to Burnsall, a picturesque village with riverbank walks. A spectacular bridge presents two options, either turn left over the bridge to visit Appletreewick or keep right to continue alongside the River Wharfe. Appletreewick is home to the Craven Arms **(9)**, recently bought by David Aynesworth, a founding director of *Folly Ales*. You are sure to receive the finest choice of this local ale served just a stone's throw from the original 'brewery' – a folly in David's garden at Burnsall.

Back to the Trail at Burnsall, where two hotels dominate the village. The Red Lion **(10)** on the banks of the Wharfe was originally a sixteenth century ferryman's Inn. Owned by the Grayshons since 1991, this is a real family affair. Beef is produced by one of the Stockdales of Burnsall, son in law to the Grayshons, and is then cooked by head chef, Jim, another son in law. Lamb comes from the Dagget family, also in the village. Local game is a speciality in season and fish is brought in daily. Beers include Greene King, Morlands, Old Speckled Hen, Theakston Best Bitter, Tetley Bitter, and another of our featured producers *Folly Ales*.

Perched on a hillside overlooking Wharfedale is the Devonshire Fell Hotel **(11)**, built as a gentleman's club for mill owners. It has undergone a transformation in recent years, since being bought by the Devonshire Estate. The décor has been overseen by the Duchess of Devonshire and the hotel is run under the superb guidance of Richard Palmer, a young man with a passion for his profession. Richard is from a farming family and works hard to ensure the hotel sources as locally as possible, supporting those farmers who frequent the premises by purchasing beef from their farms. Leaving Burnsall the trail continues along to Bolton Abbey, passing by Barden Tower. It enters the Bolton Abbey Estate and ends in the village itself, where visitors may choose to shop in the Pantry **(12)**, a delightful 'village shop' just full of produce from the area. Take home some *Stamfrey Farm Clotted Cream* and *Rosebud Preserves* to accompany the homemade scones, or buy a Sunday roast of beef or lamb from the farm of *Steven Crabtree*, one of our featured producers.

If all this seems like hard work then simply relax in the sumptuous surroundings of the Devonshire Arms Country House Hotel **(13)** where you will be served with tea in fine china, from a silver tea pot – this really is Yorkshire's answer to Claridges.

Leaving Bolton Abbey, you can choose to turn left on the A59 and join the Nidderdale Trail at Darley or turn right on the A59, passing through Skipton and on to join the Malhamdale Trail.

The Malhamdale Trail

The Malhamdale Trail commences on Malham Moor, close to the Tarn, and can be reached from either Settle, on the Ribblesdale Trail, or Arncliffe, which is in Littondale – close to the head of Wharfedale.

This is the heart of limestone country. At certain times of the year, usually between July and December, you are likely to see cattle from the *Limestone Country Beef* project grazing on the limestone pavements above the Cove. Malham Tarn (1), England's highest freshwater lake, is now part of a nature reserve area owned by the National Trust.

If you had planned a walk on your trip, this is the place to leave the car behind and enjoy the wildlife and scenery from the path along parts of the shore. Across the Tarn you will see Tarn House, a large Georgian country mansion built around 1780, which was given to the National Trust in 1946. Many influential Victorian figures of the day visited; including Charles Darwin, John Ruskin and Charles Kingsley, who wrote much of 'The Water Babies' while staying here. The house is now leased to the Field Studies Council as an educational centre.

You may prefer to leave your car in Malham village and walk up and round the Cove (2). Standing 80 metres high and 300 metres wide, this most famous of landmarks is a curved crag of limestone formed after the last Ice Age. Meltwater, particularly from Malham Tarn, cut back the Cove as it fell over the edge as a waterfall.

In Malham itself you will find several homely pubs, some wonderful bed and breakfast establishments and many really good cafes featuring locally reared, home- cooked food. The Old Barn Café (3) buys its sausages and bacon from Jackson's of Cracoe, whilst milk and eggs are from a farm in Malham and ice cream is from Brymor at Jervaulx. This is a real afternoon tea haunt with scones baked daily, amazing flapjack and the superb Yorkshire Fat Rascals.

Leave Malham on the road signposted to Skipton. Continuing through the tiny village of Kirkby Malham you will pass the church of St Michael the Archangel. Sometimes known as the 'Cathedral of the Dales', it has been here for over five hundred years. Charles Kinglsey was referring to the bells when he wrote in 'The Water Babies': 'Under the crag where the ouzel sings, And the ivied wall where the church-bell rings'.

Soon you will come to the village of Airton. Town End Farm Shop and Tea Room (4) opened in April 2003 fol-

Chris and Jane Hall have created an oasis of rural retail therapy at Town End Farm shop in Airton, a beautiful village on the main road into Malham. Turn in and purchase everyday essentials together with luxury items and eat home-cooked food in the converted barn café which upstairs houses an array of great Yorkshire gifts. Holiday cottages are also available if it is too difficult to leave.

43

Keeping his youthful looks despite all his hard work and long hours, chef director Bruce Elsworth of the Angel Inn at Hetton supports local farmers and food producers and buys regional ingredients first and foremost.

lowing conversion of a modern agricultural building. This diversification was a result of Foot and Mouth as Chris and Jane Hall had time to think about the future of farming and how they could ensure a decent living without moving away. This was a hard decision as Halls have been farming here for three generations. To fund the project they sold some land and now farm 86 acres, which support the ewes that breed the lambs they sell through the shop. A butchers' counter displays lamb from Town End Farm, alongside beef which comes from Steven Crabtree at *Bolton Abbey Foods*. Town End were one of the first retailers to sell beef from the *Limestone Country Beef* project and continue to be great supporters of this locally pro-

duced brand. They also stock a wide range of preserves from Rosebud, smoked products from Mackenzies, and an organic vegetable box scheme through *Growing with Grace*, another of our featured producers.

As you approach Gargrave you will pass the imposing Eshton Hall on your left. As the road sweeps to the right you can take a left-hand turn to Hetton and Cracoe, or continue on to Gargrave, which marks the end of the Trail. If you choose the left-hand turn the narrow, winding road takes you through the hamlet of Flasby and on to Hetton, famous as home to the Angel Inn **(5)**, a multi award winning dining pub with rooms and a wine 'cave'. Chef director Bruce Elsworth is a great supporter of local produce. Regulars on the menu here include Bolton Abbey beef and game from Alan Ellis of *Rushyford Game*. Fish is delivered daily from Fleetwood. There are two distinct dining options; the bar brasserie is cosy and informal, and here you can choose from a wide menu with dishes individually priced for you to make up your own selection – from a simple bowl of soup to a hearty three-course meal. The restaurant offers a selection of A La Carte, Table D'hote

THE MALHAMDALE TRAIL MAP KEY

❶ Malham Tarn ⓘ www.malhamdale.org.uk

❷ Malham Cove ⓘ www.malhamdale.org.uk/malham_cove

❸ Old Barn Café, *Malham, Skipton, BD23 4DA* ✆ 01729 830486 ⓘ www.malhamdale.com/oldbarn

❹ Town End Farm Shop and Café, *Scosthrop, Airton, Skipton, BD23 4BE* ✆ 01729 830902 ⓘ www.malhamdale.com/townend

❺ The Angel Inn, *Hetton, Skipton, BD23 6LT* ✆ 01756 730263 ⓘ www.angelhetton.co.uk

❻ Folly Ales, *Cracoe, Skipton, BD23 6LY* ✆ 01756 730 555 Visitors by appointment only

❼ Jacksons of Cracoe Farm Shop and Tea Room, *Cracoe, Skipton, BD23 6LB* ✆ 01756 730269 ⓘ www.jacksonsofcracoe.co.uk

❽ The Dalesman Café and Sweet Shop, *54 High Street, Gargrave, Skipton* ✆ 01756 749250

❾ Ellisons Butchers, *26 High Street, Gargrave, Skipton, BD23 3RB* ✆ 01756 749 343

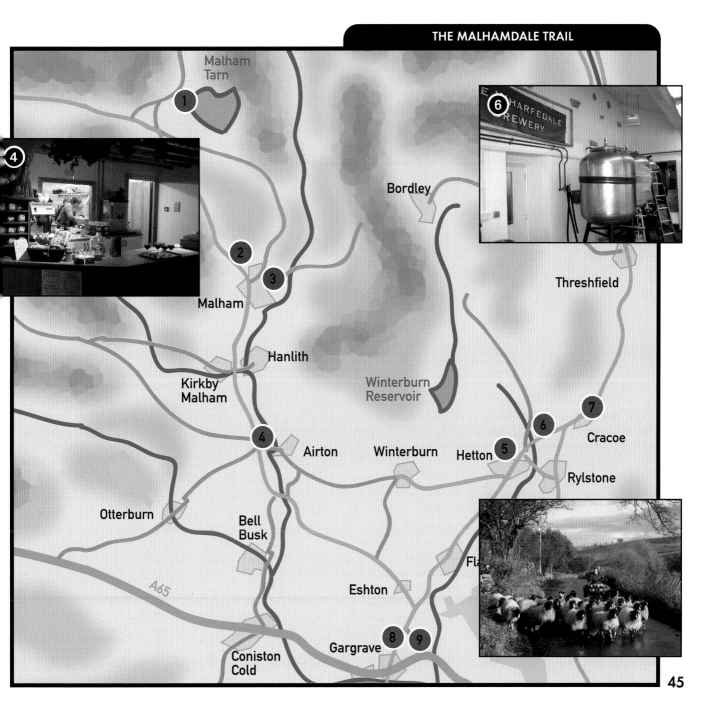

Malham
Tarn

1

4

6

Bordley

Threshfield

2

3

Malham

Hanlith

Winterburn
Reservoir

Kirkby
Malham

7

6

Cracoe

4

Airton

Winterburn

Hetton

5

Rylstone

Otterburn

Bell
Busk

Fla

Eshton

8 9

Gargrave

Coniston
Cold

A65

Bruce Elsworth at the Angel buys lamb carcasses from Bolton Abbey Foods. The cutting specification is totally to his exacting standards. His kitchen staff understand more about the food they are preparing and customers receive distinctive quality dishes on the menu, which is beneficial to farmer and chef.

and set menus. Booking is a must as this is a popular venue with visitors travelling from all over the North of England.

Moving on from the Angel the road forks at the bottom of a slight hill. Bear slightly left and follow the road to Cracoe, keeping a look out on your left for the tiny Wharfedale Brewery, home to *Folly Ales* (6). This micro brewery welcomes small groups for tours by prior arrangement. Keep straight ahead at the junction with the main Skipton to Grassington road to enter Cracoe. On a warm day you may get a waft of baking through the car window as you pass the centre of the village and the bakery of *Cottage Cakes*, sadly not open for visitors but supplying all the local farmers markets.

Next stop is Jackson's Farm Shop (7), a family run business, tea room and butchers selling award-winning sausages, made on the premises from locally sourced pork. Jackson's, who also supply many other outlets featured in these pages, were one of the very first farm shops in the Dales. They have been open for almost twenty-five years and are a superb example of how a retail outlet can support local farmers and growers. They are licensed game dealers, supplying venison, grouse, wood pigeons and pheasant in season, alongside locally fed beef, lamb and pork. In the summer months we recommend taking home one of their barbecue specials - everything you need, including local charcoal!

From Cracoe you may continue on to Threshfield and join the Wharfedale Trail or return to Gargrave to complete the Malhamdale Trail with afternoon tea at the Dalesman (8), a pretty little café in the centre of the village. Their publicity states that they welcome 'Walkers, Cyclists and Civilians'!

If you don't have time to stop for tea, do pop into Ellisons (9), the wonderful family butcher located on the High Street, where Dennis and Thelma pride themselves on selling meat from local farms. Dennis was one of the last local butchers to go on to farms to choose his own beasts, although they now buy from a local abattoir that is used by farmers in the area. This is a real family affair; the shop was recently divided into two and the couple's son Adam, who trained as a butcher first, has opened a fish and chip shop next door. The village had been without this facility for a couple of years since the old established 'chippy' was sold for development. Thelma is responsible for making the pastry that tops their famous pork pies – and for keeping the men in line! Ian, who has worked in the shop for as long as most people can remember, is a constant source of inspiration. I often wander in mid-afternoon with no idea of what to do for tea and always come away with not only delicious locally reared meat but a recipe for it too.

The Ribblesdale Trail

The Ribblesdale Trail starts out at Clapham, where you may be joining en-route from Scotland or the Lake District as the A65 is the main route from the Lakes to the Dales. A relatively small village, Clapham is home to two of the area's most valued organisations. The Cave Rescue Organisation provides the cave and mountain rescue service in the Three Peaks area of the Yorkshire Dales National Park, and also in parts of Lancashire and Cumbria as well as eastwards as far as Malhamdale. The Yorkshire Dales Millennium Trust was set up in 1998 to facilitate and fund projects that conserve the Dales.

Heading south-east down the A65 look out for roadside signs in the form of three carrot- shaped windsocks that point to *Growing with Grace* (1), one of our featured producers. A little further on you will come to the turning for Austwick. Situated in the lower part of Crummackdale the village benefits from its slightly elevated position and enjoys spectacular views of limestone crags.

Austwick is clearly signed from the A65 and is about halfway between Clapham and Settle. This is a great place to stop off for morning coffee, lunch or afternoon tea and it fits well into a journey that might also take in Settle, Skipton, Malhamdale or Hawes. Travelling on the A65, you are following the traditional Romany Trail to Appleby Horse Fair. The 'traders' stopped off at Austwick en-route and much dealing took place here in the Traddock – short for Trading Paddock. Now a beautiful country house hotel, the Austwick Traddock (2) is not only

(Left) A welcome sight on the A65. Softening the big metal barrier, Growing with Grace paint it bright yellow and add a friendly sign.
(Right) On a cold Clapham morning, Growing With Grace offers warmth and security in the glasshouses and poly tunnels, where a variety of vegetables, herbs and salads grow in abundance.

committed to sourcing its produce locally but is one for the first hotel restaurants in the country to achieve full organic certification.

You can select from a wonderful choice of wild game in season, provided by Alan Ellis of *Rushyford Game*, and there is always organic lamb, pork or beef from *Fresh from the Farm*, another of our featured producers. Puds and afternoon teas are complemented by organic clotted cream from *Stamfrey Farm* and salad leaves will have travelled the short distance from *Growing with Grace*.

If you have time for a walk in Austwick do take the road up to Feizor. This steep winding track will take in some of the most spectacular limestone scenery in the Dales and along the way you may spot Jonathon Knowle's herd of Herefords grazing here as part of the *Limestone Country Beef* project.

Travelling south you will soon be in Settle, an historic town with a market each Tuesday and host on the first Sunday in the month to *Northern Dales Farmers Markets*. The Market Place in Settle is tucked under the shadow towering Catlebergh, a majestic outcrop of limestone rock, and there are a series of streets and 'ginnels' leading off from here. Explore these and you will find hidden gems such as Poppies tea room, with cakes and savouries made with produce from the region. Daisy Fresh (3) is a wonderful deli which prepares its own cooked meats on site and stocks a fabulous range of products including flour from *Sunflours*, ice cream, cheese and clotted cream from Brymor and organic beef and lamb from *Fresh from the Farm*.

Situated at the head of the Market Place is the wonderful family butchers Drake and Macefield with shops in both Skipton and Settle. Business partners Ian Thompson and Richard Teal have won many awards over the years and have even netted the supreme accolade for the best stand

RECIPE: Traditional Meat & Potato Pie

For this dish we asked Robert Phillips of Hellifield Highlanders to provide small, diced, pieces of shin beef. The flavour was already superb, and it could only be ever so slightly improved by adding half a pint of Folly Ale to the meat once sealed.

500g (1lb) shin beef, cut into small pieces
25g (1oz) seasoned flour
25g (1oz) butter
250g (8oz) short crust pastry
1 large onion, cut up
1 fresh bay leaf
Salt and pepper
1kg (2lb) potatoes

Pre-heat oven to 190 degrees/Gas mark 5. Roll the beef in the seasoned flour. Melt the butter in a pan and when sizzling add the beef to seal. Add 1 pint of water, onion and bay leaf and simmer for one and a half hours until tender. Boil the potatoes, cut into chunks, and add to the meat. Put into a pie dish, add a little stock, then cover with fairly thick short crust pastry. Bake in a hot oven for forty minutes. Use the remaining meat stock to make a gravy. Serve with mash and seasonal vegetables. Red cabbage is delicious with a Meat and Potato Pie.

THE RIBBLESDALE TRAIL MAP KEY

1 Growing with Grace, *Clapham Nursery, Clapham, Lancaster, LA2 8ER* © 01524 251723 ⓘ www.growingwithgrace.co.uk

2 The Austwick Traddock, *Austwick, Lancaster, LA2 8BY* © 01524 251224 ⓘ www.austwicktraddock.co.uk

3 Daisy Fresh Deli, *8 High Street, Settle, BD24 9EX* T 01729 822 834

4 Horton In Ribblesdale Post Office, *Main Street, Horton-in-Ribblesdale, Settle, BD24 0HD* © 01729 860232 ⓘ www.hortonpostoffice.co.uk

5 Layhead Farm Cottages, *Field House, Rathmell, Settle, BD24 0LA* © 01729 840234 ⓘ www.layhead.co.uk *Bookings or visitors by appointment*

6 The Plough, *Wigglesworth, Settle, BD23 4RJ* © 01729 840243 ⓘ sue@ploughinn.info www.ploughinn.info

7 Hellifield Highland Beef, *Green Farm, Hellifield, Skipton, BD23 4LA* © 01729 850217 ⓘ www.hellifieldhighlanders.co.uk *Visitors by appointment only*

8 Coniston Hotel, *Coniston Cold, Skipton, BD23 4EB* © 01756 748080 ⓘ info@theconistonhotel.com www.theconistonhotel.com

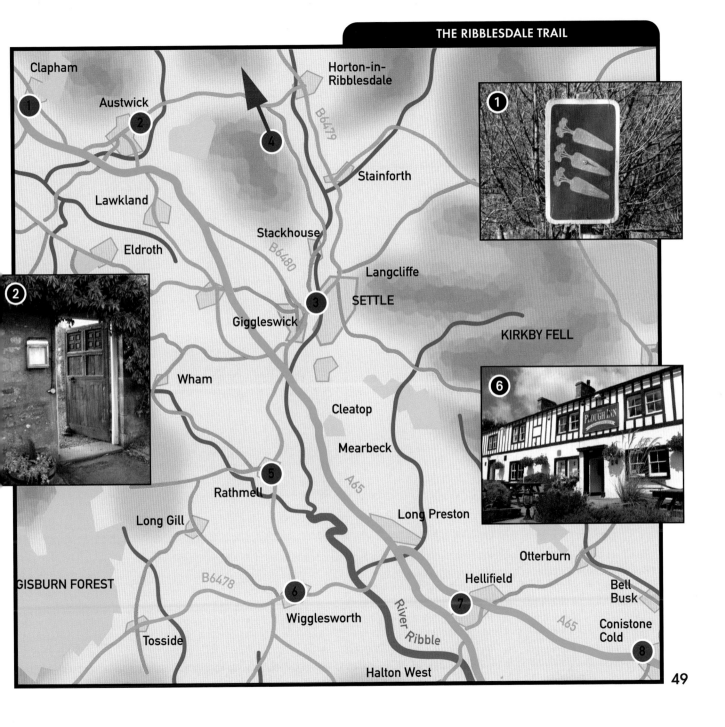

Clapham

Austwick

Horton-in-Ribblesdale

Stainforth

Lawkland

Stackhouse

Eldroth

Langcliffe

SETTLE

Giggleswick

KIRKBY FELL

Wham

Cleatop

Mearbeck

Rathmell

Long Preston

Long Gill

Otterburn

GISBURN FOREST

Hellifield

Bell Busk

Wigglesworth

River Ribble

Conistone Cold

Tosside

Halton West

B6479

B6480

B6478

A65

A65

49

(Left) And so to bed – in the beautiful country house hotel that is the Austwick Traddock.
(Right) The hotel's well-managed and calm kitchen produces deliciously tasting organic food as well as service with style and a smile.

pie in the entire country. This happened when they were awarded the large pork pie championship at the 2003 National Pie & Pasty Competition. The two are highly supportive of local producers, being one of the first butchers in the area to sell beef from the Limestone Country project, and are always sourcing produce locally for both shops.

You may have arrived in Settle from the Wensleydale Trail, via the B6479 from Hawes, in which case you will have travelled through Horton in Ribblesdale, passing the award winning Post Office and Village Store **(4)**. This well stocked shop is also a haven for 'foodies', making up boxes to greet holidaymakers and stocking such delights as preserves from *Rosebud*, Ribblesdale cheese and smoked meats from Mackenzies.

At this point you are right in the heart of the Three Peaks, with Ingleborough to your right and Pen-y-Ghent to your left. Ingleborough is home to the English Nature herd of *Limestone Country Beef* cattle. The nature reserve was awarded the Euro Sites 2000 award for conservation, indicating that not only do these cattle produce some of the best beef you will ever taste but are also preserving the landscape for future generations to enjoy.

If you choose to continue south on the A65 it is worth taking a detour to Wigglesworth. The road winds along the Ribble Valley through Rathmell, where you will pass by the Northern Equine Therapy Centre, already noted as a successful farm diversification project. Layhead Farm Cottages (5) in Rathmell provide extensive, dog friendly, holiday accommodation, ideal for larger families and groups, and also offer meals by prior arrangement.

The meals are provided by Bendgate, a new catering company from Long Preston totally committed to sourcing locally and providing a wide range of exciting produce. Their beef pie, featuring choice cuts of meat from *Steven Crabtree* of Bolton Abbey, is just wonderful. Another particular favourite is the BIG Breakfast cereal, a collection of fruit and grains smothered in local honey and carrying the warning, 'This is not a diet food, if you want to loose weight eat less and walk further'. All of the products produced by Bendgate carry some sort of message, making them fun to buy as well as delicious to eat. Bendgate can be seen at many local shows and events or why not request a menu from which to select from for home delivery (tel 01729 850659; www.bendgate.com).

Leaving Rathmell you may notice the farm of *Adrian Proctor* on the right hand side. Although this is not an 'open farm' Adrian does welcome visitors by prior arrangement. A little further along the road you will arrive at the Plough Inn (6), established in 1750 when an enterprising farmer's wife began to sell ale from her kitchen. The inn now offers a wide choice of local produce. A particular feature of the Plough is the 'War of the Roses' – they record every order for Yorkshire Pudding and Lancashire Hot Pot and keep a running total over the bar! Recently they have started to feature a menu totally dedicated to the great British sausage with flavours to suit all palates.

You will re-join the A65 at Hellifield where you can't fail to see the fields full of Highland cattle. Robert Phillip of Hellifield Highlanders (7) sells beef direct from the farm and many of these beautiful beasts are grazed as part of the *Limestone Country Beef* project, spending much of their

Local organic lamb from the nearby Fresh From the Farm is cooked with joy at the Plough Inn, Wigglesworth, by David the chef and his team. Turn up for a possible real life 'meet the producer' as farmer Adrian is also a regular at the bar

time on the limestone pavements above Malham Cove.

Our Trail ends at Coniston Cold, where you can stop off at the Coniston Hotel (8) for morning coffee, afternoon tea, lunch or dinner. In summer this can be taken outside on the patio, with spectacular views across the lake to Malhamdale, and on a winter's day by a roaring log fire in the bar. The Bannister family have transformed and added to a redundant farm building, growing from a small farm shop to a fifty-bedroom hotel that provides a wonderful local employment opportunity. Under the careful guidance of their youngest son Tom the hotel has gained an excellent reputation for the quality of the food and service is always with a smile.

Just a few miles further south you can join the start of the Malhamdale Trail in the village of Gargrave on the banks of the River Aire.

The Wensleydale Trail

The Wensleydale Trail starts at Hawes and you could quite happily spend at least half a day sampling the wonderful range of produce both made and on sale in this market town. The name, Hawes, means a 'pass between mountains', and it stands between Buttertubs and Fleet Moss.

Hawes is probably most famous for being home to the Wensleydale Creamery (1), now enjoying worldwide acclaim thanks to the recommendations of Wallace and Gromit. The dairy has a colourful past, dating back to 1897 when Edward Chapman began to purchase milk from surrounding farms to use for the manufacture of Wensleydale cheese. The industrial depression of the 1930s made trading conditions difficult and the dairy was facing closure.

Wensleydale farmers, who were owed money by the dairy, were offered contracts by the Milk Marketing Board to take Dales milk to a national dairy miles away. The farmers were adamant that the Hawes dairy should continue and in 1935 they found a champion of their cause in Kit Calvert. He called a meeting in the Town Hall and gathered enough support to rescue the dairy. However, this was not the end of the tale as the Milk Marketing Board recognised its potential and in 1966 purchased Wensleydale Creamery. In May 1992 Dairy Crest, a subsidiary of the Board, closed the creamery and transferred production of Wensleydale cheese to Lancashire! The ex-managers took up the fight and, against the odds, eventually persuaded the owners to sell the creamery to them. A management buy-out was agreed in November 1992. Many of that original team are still in place today with production overseen by Alice Amsden, who is also a leading light in Swaledale Sheep circles.

Wensleydale Creamery now boasts a comprehensive visitor centre, which is open every day except Christmas Day. Visitors can experience the cheese-making process, although it should be noted that cheese is not made every day and you should check ahead if you particularly want to include that element in your visit. There is a tea room, bar and shop, where visitors are invited to sample a selection of the many cheeses produced on site. As well as the traditional white Wensleydale or the famous blue-veined, try some of the fruit or herb-infused varieties. Alternatively, take home a selection of 'minis' which include the ewes' milk Wensleydale and the Garsdale, a garlic and chive variety suitable for vegetarians.

The Creamery has teamed up with another of the North's leading producers, Elizabeth Botham of Whitby,

Inside Elijah Allen's it is possible to fulfil almost any culinary need – along with many food products you might not have known you 'needed'! It is almost impossible to leave without buying something and be really happy about it. If every village or town had a shop like this the world would be a happier place.

to offer a pack of that tantalising favourite, Wensleydale cheese and fruit cake. We have not seen the latest Wallace and Gromit film yet but if they haven't yet discovered this most delicious combination we must tell them they are missing out!

There are several excellent eating places in Hawes. Herriot's Hotel (2) features local lamb on the menu, alongside an excellent blue Wensleydale tartlet. Cocketts Hotel (3) can boast having had the same chef for over fifteen years – he sources locally with meat coming from Bainbridge and with Wensleydale quite properly featuring on the cheeseboard. The White Hart Inn (4) features fillet steak supplied by its neighbouring butcher JW Cockett & Son – no relation to the hoteliers we are told.

Don't leave Hawes without a visit to Elijah Allen (5), undoubtedly the finest traditional grocers in the Dales. It is a real step back in time where friendly traditional service is delivered effortlessly by a team of knowledgeable staff. They work under the watchful eye of owner Richard Allen, with help from his father Basil, now retired, and sister Lesley when she manages time away from her own family

(Left) The culprit of temptation at Raydale Preserves can be found on the stove bubbling away in the spotless production kitchen, which still retains a hint of its rustic rural roots. An old cow shed now doubles as kitchen and storeroom and is a lovely place to visit and purchase these special preserves.

(Right) The Kettlewell's welcoming home is where Raydale Preserves all started, although jam and chutney production has now moved to the converted barn next door. Tastings take place in the old schoolhouse and village hall the other side of the house. During simmering time the whole area becomes enveloped in a fruity sugary aroma that takes attention away from the fantastic landscape.

business, Raydale Preserves.

Elijah Allen was established in 1860 by Richard's great, great grandfather Thomas, who was a farmer in the area and also had carts that were hired out for funerals and weddings! This must be one of the first-ever examples of farm diversification, as Thomas filled his carts with supplies and rode over the hill to Ribblehead where the navvies building the railway viaduct were excellent customers. The farmhouse soon became a shop and the business moved to its present site in 1910.

As well as shelves stacked high with all manner of local-ly produced goods, there is an in-house bakery producing breads, cakes and pastries. Local meats are cooked on site to fill a deli counter that also includes over twenty cheeses from Wensleydale Creamery as well as other local varieties such as Swaledale. To accompany, there is a huge selection of cheese biscuits, home-baked oatcakes, flour from *Sunflours* of Grewelthorpe, milk from Askrigg, biscuits from Whitby, the fabulous Cartmel sticky toffee pudding and an extensive range of Raydale preserves.

Leaving Hawes on the A684 the next village along is Bainbridge. However, if visiting between May and October it is worth making a detour to take in the breath-

THE WENSLEYDALE TRAIL MAP KEY

❶ Wensleydale Creamery and Visitor Centre, *Gayle Lane, Hawes, DL8 3RN* ℂ 01969 667664 W www.wensleydale.co.uk

❷ Herriots Hotel, *Main Street, Hawes, DL8 3QW* ℂ 01969 667536 ⓘ www.herriotsinhawes.co.uk

❸ Cocketts Hotel, *Market Place, Hawes, DL8 3RD* ℂ 01969 667312

❹ White Hart Inn, *Main Street, Hawes, DL8 3QL* ℂ 01969 667 259

❺ Elijah Allen, *Market Place, Hawes, DL8 3Q* ℂ 01969 667219

❻ Raydale Preserves, *School House Farm, Stalling Busk, Leyburn, DL8 3DH* ℂ 01969 650233 *Open seasonally*

❼ Sticky Ginger, *Market Place, Askrigg, Leyburn, DL8 3HL* ℂ 01969 650049 ⓘ www.sticky-ginger.co.uk

❽ Wensleydale Heifer, *West Witton, DL8 4LS* ℂ 01969 622322 ⓘ www.wensleydaleheifer.co.uk

❾ The Little Chocolate Shop, *3A Herriot Court, Leyburn Business Park, Leyburn, DL8 5QA.* ℂ 01969 625288 ⓘ www.thelittlechoco-lateshop.co.uk

❿ The Teapottery, *Leyburn Business Park, Leyburn, DL8 5QA* ℂ 01937 582244 ⓘ www.teapot-tery.co.uk

⓫ Black Swan, *Market Place, Middleham, DL8 4NP* ℂ 01969 622221 ⓘ www.middlehamon-line.com

⓬ Brymor Ice cream Farm and Parlour, *A.B. Moore Farmers Ltd, High Jervaulx Farm, Masham, HG4 4PG* ℂ 01677 460377 ⓘ www.abmoore.co.uk

⓭ The Masham Sausage Shop, *11 Silver Street, Masham, Ripon* ℂ 01765 640099 ⓘ www.mashamsausages.co.uk

⓮ Bah Humbugs, *12 The Market Place, Masham, Ripon, HG4 4EB* ℂ 01765 688 997 ⓘ www.bah-humbugs.com

⓯ Joneva, *Market Place, 7 Market Place, Masham* ℂ 01765 689 021 ⓘ www.joneva.com

⓰ The Black Sheep Brewery Plc, *Wellgarth, Masham, Ripon, HG4 4EN* ℂ 01765 689227 ⓘ www.black-sheep.co.uk

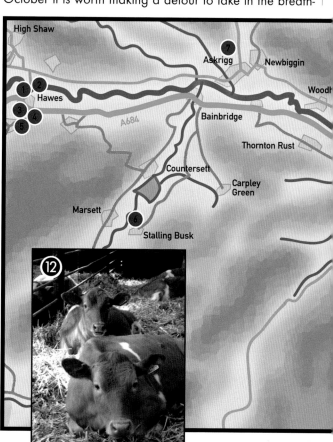

taking scenery around Semerwater and stop at Stalling Busk, the home of Raydale Preserves **(6)**. Raydale is owned by Derrick and Lesley Kettlewell. Lesley, the sister of Richard Allen of Elijah Allen, married Derrick, a local farmer whose family have farmed here since the 1940s. Stalling Busk is little more than a collection of ten houses. Sadly, only three are now occupied full time, the remainder being holiday and second homes, but for those who are lucky enough to have secured a property in this area where better for complete isolation and relaxation?

Raydale make preserves the old fashioned way, in small six-kilogram batches, incorporating locally grown fruits and vegetables with herbs from their own garden. The range is extensive, from traditional Victoria Plum Jam through to some truly creative additions – Lime and Pernod Jelly, Blackcurrant and Vodka Jelly – and back to a gentler sounding Summer Fruits Jam. New additions include Raydale Mustard, incorporating local ale, and Elizabethan Mustard, made from an old family recipe and perfect for coating a gammon before roasting.

Recently the farm has undergone further diversification, with the addition of Raydale Rambles, five specially

THE WENSLEYDALE TRAIL

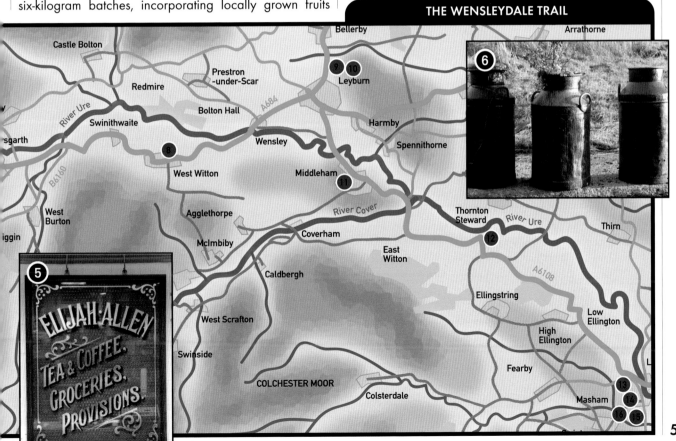

Temper temper! Tempering is what is needed to enable the perfect crack of bite and smooth melt in the mouth. At the Little Chocolate shop in Leyburn it is possible to watch it happening, learn all about it and treat yourself on the way out.

designed conservation walks that take in the spectacular scenery of the area and have been designed to appeal to all levels of ability. In preparation for the walk you may take refreshments in the newly opened tea and tasting room, which happens to be in the old schoolroom, adjoining the farmhouse. Any resemblance to a village hall is entirely correct as it also serves as a community facility for the use of local residents.

Passing through Bainbridge you may notice signs for Askgrigg, the location of Skeldale House which was used as a base for James Herriot in the long running BBC series 'All Creatures Great and Small'. The Kings Arms will be remembered as the Drovers Arms. On the main street visit Sticky Ginger (7), a relatively new deli and café serving home-cooked food throughout the day. Richard and Julie Blowes have built a thriving business and are well known for their sumptuous food parcels delivered to holiday homes throughout the dale. Pick up preserves from Raydale or an ice cream from Brymor or collect a full meal to enjoy at home. You can be sure it will contain only fresh, locally produced ingredients.

En route to Leyburn you will pass through West Witton, where the Wensleydale Heifer (8) has been taken over by new owners with a team of chefs who hail from some of the best seafood restaurants in the north of England. As you would expect the menu does lean heavily towards the coastal regions and this is a superb opportunity to experience fish brought in fresh every day from Whitby. We felt we had to include an excerpt from the hotel's website: 'The Heifer is pleased to announce that it has secured fresh Monday fish deliveries. Whitby fisherman, Phil Menetup, said, "It's been reet 'ard to get t' fish in t' net and then in t' waggon but we med it in t' end."'

Next stop is Leyburn, another small market town just bursting with opportunities to sample and buy fantastic food. We highly recommend visiting the well-established Leyburn Festival of Food and Drink which takes place on the outskirts of the town on May Bank Holiday each year. Over a hundred local producers gather to create a tented village that resembles the finest of food halls with a touch of reality. There are cookery and farming demonstrations and refreshments to suit all tastes. It was here we saw cheese being made, sampled garlic-flavoured honey and milked a cardboard cow, provided by the NFU to remind children of the source of milk.

At other times of the year we recommend a visit to the Little Chocolate Shop (9). This interesting visitor centre has already needed to move twice since its launch in a basement kitchen in 2001. Learn about the history of chocolate and watch one of the demonstrations that run throughout the day. Close by the Chocolate Shop is the Tea Pottery (10), a well-known visitor attraction making tea pots of all shapes and sizes. Leyburn is well served by a range of pubs, tea rooms and cafes, some of which serve local produce. On the fourth Saturday of the month arrive early to be sure to see the full range of local produce available from the farmers market, run to the highest standards by Alastair Davy of *Northern Dales Farmers Markets*. On most Thursdays between 10am and 11.30am there is the Wensleydale country market, a sale of home-baking and produce fresh from the garden.

To continue on the Wensleydale Trail, take the A6108 out of Leyburn heading towards Middleham. Alternatively, you can go the opposite direction, signed for Richmond, and join the Swaledale Trail.

If you stay with the Wensleydale Trail the next town is Middleham, dominated by the imposing remains of a large medieval castle once the home of King Richard III. Middleham is well known as a centre for racehorse training and you would be extremely unlucky to pass through without getting a glimpse in to this fascinating and elegant sport. There are some fifteen training establishments and Middleham now boasts its own grass and all-weather gallops on the Low and High Moors.

The Black Swan (11) in Middleham serves superb home-cooked food and supports local producers all the way. Select from a range of fabulous sausages from the Masham Sausage shop. Hog and Hop, Country Herb, pork and gluten free sausages are all regulars on the bar menu, or for a more substantial meal visit the restaurant where the meat is from Cockburn's Family Butchers in Bedale.

Nearing the close of the Wensleydale Trail with just Masham to go, you may like to pause for refreshments at High Jervaulx Farm, the relatively new home of Brymor Ice Cream (12). The business was originally established in

Beavers Butchers from where the famous Masham Sausages started. It is well worth a stop to stock up on delicious prize-winning sausages, fresh or for the freezer.

1984, when milk quotas were introduced. The Moore family then farmed at Weeton in Lower Wharfedale, but Brymor outgrew the original farm and, following a two-year search, the family moved to this beautiful location, close to Jervaulx Abbey, where Wensleydale cheese was first produced.

This is one of Britain's few genuine on-farm manufactures where only milk produced on the premises is used in the production of the ice cream. Noted for its spacious ice cream parlour, it is a real family affair run by founders **57**

Joneva is a jolly shop situated right by the car park in Masham so it is almost impossible not to be tempted. Once inside there is a sweet or chocolate to suit every occasion, pocket, craving or mood. With the deli at the back, both savoury and sweet tooths will be satisfied and the friendly team delight in it all with you.

Brian and Brenda's son, Robert, and his wife Diane, whilst employing three generations of Moores plus full and part time staff. During the summer months you will see the gorgeous herd of Guernsey cows grazing on the lush green pastures that surround the farm. In chillier times they are to be found loose housed on straw in the barns that run alongside the parlour car park.

Finally to Masham and the end of the Wensleydale Trail. In this delightful market town with wonderful Georgian architecture, you will find a host of 'foodie' shops to satisfy every possible taste. A visit to the Masham Sausage Shop **(13)** is a must. Co-founder Richard Welford has been in the family business all his working life, taking over from his grandfather sixteen years ago. Richard started specialising in sausages nine years ago and has won thirty different awards. The business, which has gone from strength to strength, now supplies Betty's Tea Rooms. There

are currently forty varieties of sausage, from the standard pork, still a favourite with children of all ages, through to some local delicacies. These include 'Hog and Hop' featuring Black Sheep ale, a festive Turkey and Apple and a gourmet Duck and Orange. Don't worry if you can't take them all home – they do a fast and efficient mail order service, ensuring that visitors to the dale can enjoy Masham Sausages wherever they are.

Masham has plenty to satisfy those with a sweet tooth, with a visit to Bah Humbugs **(14)** being a trip back in time. Local girl Lucy Scott-Paul opened the shop in 2004, encouraged by friends who were keen to experience again such delights as 'Parma Violets' and aniseed balls – the ones with the pip! There is everything from cherry lips to sherbet pips and plenty of modern day additions too. Just across the Market Place stands the chocoholic's paradise that is Joneva **(15)**, selling the very finest Belgium chocolates along with many locally produced deli products too.

Beer buffs will be spoilt for choice here with two of the North's most famous breweries vying for attention. Moreover they are on each other's doorsteps – in fact one moved into premises vacated by another. Theakston Brewery was founded in a hotel on Silver Street in 1827. Following a short period in the ownership of Scottish and Newcastle, heirs of the original founder, Robert Theakston, bought back the company in 2003 and it continues to produce some wonderful beer at its Masham site. Theakstons employ the last apprenticed craft cooper in the country, Jonathon Manby, who can be seen crafting traditional oak barrels. In 1992 Black Sheep **(16)**, owned by Paul and Sue Theakston, began brewing ales that in a short period of time have become some of the most popular beers produced by any independent brewery. It offers tours and has an on-site shop selling the ales and associated products.

As you would expect from a town with such a strong brewing industry, there are several beer festivals throughout the year. In September both locals and visitors enjoy the annual sheep fair.

The Swaledale Trail

One of the best parts of writing this book, apart from meeting so many wonderful farmers and growers, was having the luxury of time to savour the amazing scenery which, living in such a beautiful area, we all too often take for granted. This was brought home more than ever when we visited Swaledale. In the past I have been to Richmond but the journey through Swaledale was nothing short of inspirational. There is something almost unreal about the landscape here – if Swaledale were a painting it would be a Monet.

For those brave enough you can join the Swaledale Trail via the spectacular Buttertubs pass – an unclassified road that runs from Hardraw, close to Hawes on the Wensleydale Trail. Turn right once over the pass and join the B6270 to head down-dale through Gunnerside. Alternatively take the A6108 from Leyburn to Richmond. We will start the Trail at Low Row and conclude just above Richmond at Gilling West, which is very handy for the A1.

Hazel Brow (1) is typical of most farms in Swaledale where lead mining was once a thriving industry. Families would farm a small area of land, keeping a few sheep, cows and a pig. Animals were tended by the womenfolk and children and were housed close to dwellings or in field barns. This farming system has left us with the unique landscape we have today. The Calvert family farm 93 hectares of land and through the summer months the cattle graze shared common land around and above the village. Melbecks Moor similarly provides shared grazing for the flock of Swaledale sheep. Hazel Brow is a truly mixed

The stunning backdrop of the Swaledale fells is an integral part of the idyllic community of Reeth. The village is also a splendid place to sample great food and drink in its pubs, hotels, shops and cafes.

This man's moist fruitcake is to die for! From his immaculate kitchen he produces gorgeous food for residents of the Burgoyne Country House Hotel and passers-by, all sourced locally and of the highest quality.

farm, with forty-five Friesian milking cows as well as beef cattle and their calves. The five hundred hardy Swaledale sheep are native to the area and are able to survive the cold snowy winters on the moors. They are 'hefted', meaning they have their own territory to which they return each year. The farm also has an assortment of pigs, hens, ducks and geese that are kept for home produce.

In 2002 the Calverts converted to organic farming and have recently opened a café to complement the visitor centre, which serves organic meals and drinks. Home-made

cakes and scones, filled rolls and hot soup, cold drinks and ice creams are available, together with some great new recipes including 'haytime lemonade' and Swaledale Shepherds Pie. The visitor centre is open from the end of March until the end of September. Each day includes a packed programme of activities for all the family, with plenty to do even in wet weather. The nature trail takes you away from the farm buildings to the river Swale, along the riverbank and back to the farm. There is also a series of walks from the farm, ranging from reasonably gentle through to quite challenging; maps are available, along with a hearty packed lunch to send you on your way.

Moving on, we followed the beautiful valley road and arrived in Reeth, historically a centre for hand-knitting. The Swaledale lead industry was controlled from here, but it was always a market town for the local farming community. The market is still held each Friday in the centre of the village. Reeth is popular with tourists and we were greeted by a vast array of tea rooms, all serving wonderful local produce. Out here they have little choice as the large wholesalers would not find it viable to deliver to such a

THE SWALEDALE TRAIL MAP KEY

❶ Hazel Brow Farm and Visitor Centre, *Low Row, Richmond, DL11 6NE* ✆ 01748 886224 ⓘ info@hazelbrow.co.uk www.hazelbrow.co.uk *Open seasonally*

❷ Garden House – Damson cheese, *The Garden House, Anvil Square, Reeth, Richmond, North Yorkshire DL11 6TE* ✆ 01748 884188

❸ Burgoyne Hotel, *On the Green, Reeth, Richmond, DL11 6SN* ✆ 01748 884292 ⓘ www.the-burgoyne.co.uk

❹ Frenchgate Hotel, *59-61*

Frenchgate, Richmond, DL10 4HZ ✆ 01748 822 087

❺ New Frenchgate café bar, *Frenchgate, Richmond, DL10 4HZ* ✆ 01748 824 949

❻ Bluebell Organics, *Forcett Hall Walled Gardens, Forcett, Richmond, DL11 7SB* ✆ 01325 718841 ⓘ www.bluebellorganics.co.uk *Visitors by arrangement*

❼ Mainsgill Farm shop, *Gilling West, Richmond, DL11 7PN* ✆ 01325 718385 ⓘ www.mainsgillfarm.co.uk

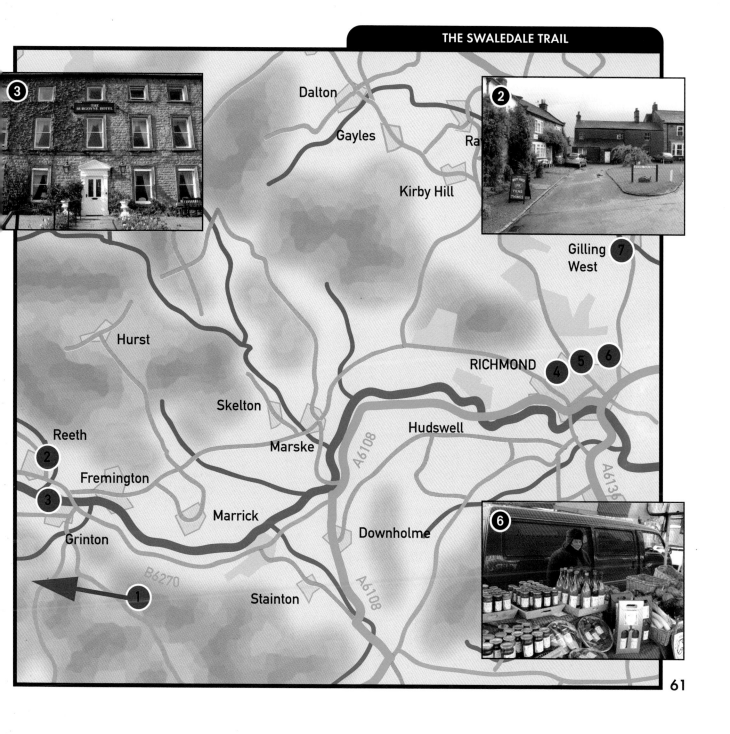

3

2

Dalton

Gayles

Ra

Kirby Hill

Gilling
West 7

Hurst

RICHMOND 4 5 6

Reeth

Skelton

Hudswell

2

Marske

A6108

Fremington

3

Marrick

Downholme

Grinton

A6108

A6136

B6270

1

Stainton

6

Bright, cheerful and full of goodness, a meal at the New Frenchgate is a relaxing epicurean affair where quality and traceability is the norm. Customers benefit from the dedication and hard work of the small team in turning great local produce into tempting exciting food.

rural outpost. We were on a mission to find Garden House Pottery **(2)**, the home of the award- winning Damson Cheese – and what a find! Jane and Ray Davies, who were looking for ways of using their glut of damsons, have come up with a perfect solution. Ray, a potter, makes reusable pottery bowls that are used by Jane for her dam-

son cheese. Jane came across the recipe when Ray gave her an old cookbook called 'Food in England'. In the introduction was a passage describing Victorian dinner parties in gentrified Yorkshire circles, and ever since then their square oak-beamed office and storeroom has each January become the production line for one of the most exclusive products in the country. Over 700lbs of damsons go into making this delectable product, which is actually not a cheese at all – it is a robust and exciting pudding! It can be served with clotted cream, crème fraiche or ice cream, but just to confuse matters it has the consistency of a smooth pate and is an excellent accompaniment to game, lamb or fine cheeses.

The damsons are grown in their own orchard and are harvested and frozen every September. In January – when tourism in the village of Reeth has tailed off – Jane will prepare the fruit, meticulously cleaning each damson. It's quite intensive, but the work is over by February. After cleaning the damsons, Jane heats them gently in the oven until the fruits burst. They are then sieved coarsely to remove the stones before putting them through a finer sieve to make a thick purée. This is then heated, stirred and tweaked until the right consistency is achieved. However, the 'cheese' will not be ready for consumption until April, by which time it will have set into a firm, purple-black jelly that will last for years and will be at its very best when sugar begins to crystallise on its surface.

In need of refreshment we headed across the village green to the Burgoyne Hotel **(3)**, a late Georgian country house hotel, upgraded in a very traditional style by owners Peter Cawardine and Derek Hickson, who, having made a success of various hotels and eateries around the Dales, finally settled here ten years ago. Peter is a nationally acclaimed chef whilst Derek presides over 'front of house' – and a wonderful team they make. We took afternoon tea in front of a huge inglenook fireplace, joined occasionally by the resident dog. From our seats we had a perfect view of the garden gate and were fascinated to see a member of the team from *Swaledale Cheese* making one of their regular deliveries – by bicycle! Peter and Derek are great supporters, featuring the Swaledale Sheep's Cheese and Blue Cheese on the dinner menus.

Departing refreshed we continued along the B6270, following the line of the River Swale and eventually arriving in Richmond. An historic market town with Norman castle and Georgian architecture, it also has a cobbled market place, monuments and a nearby abbey, the fast flowing river and breathtaking scenery. Again there is no shortage of tea rooms, cafes, restaurants and hotels to suit all tastes and budgets. Frenchgate is particularly well served with both the Frenchgate Hotel (4) and the New Frenchgate (5), each supporting local producers and each with individual style. At the Frenchgate Hotel guests can relax in the residents lounge, a tranquil early seventeenth-century room where the original heavy oak beams are complemented by the beautifully carved woodwork of the noted craftsman Robert Thompson, the 'Mouseman of Kilburn'. The New Frenchgate is a vibrant café bar serving tapas and more traditional snacks throughout the day and into the evening. We were delighted to find it listing its local suppliers on the menu. Meat is from Mainsgill Farm Shop and cheese from Swaledale. Ice cream is from Brymor and specialist whole foods come from The Wives Kitchen, a well-established business in the town that also supplies a large range of health foods catering for people on special diets.

Nearing the end of this Trail we took a detour from the main A6108, following the B6274 to Gilling West and Mainsgill Farm Shop (7), home for the past eleven years to Andrew and Maria Henshaw, who moved here as a newly married couple to run a farm. Realising from an early stage that they would have to diversify to survive, they started to sell meat from the farm direct to local catering establishments and to local people. The business has now grown to such an extent that they employ three full time butchers on site. There is a well-stocked farm shop,

Along with other hearty foods, Mainsgill Farm produces and sells great meat – and also passionately promotes the best ways of cooking it. Buying a decent sized joint for a Sunday family roast can be the basis of many meals throughout the week.

which also supports other local producers. Here you can buy cheese from Swaledale and Wensleydale, Raydale preserves, ice cream from Brymor and the superb *Stamfrey Farm Clotted Cream* and newly launched organic yoghurt. Inside the shop is a busy tea room serving light meals throughout the day. Enjoy award winning sausages, or take home one of the wonderful home-made cakes, also winners of many awards including gold at the Guild of Fine Food Retailers 'great taste' awards.

It is not only the farm that has grown as Andrew and Maria now have three children, aged from four up to nine. Each has their role on the farm – the favourite job is feeding the llamas and alpacas. With so much going on it is not surprising that Mainsgill recently won a 'Farm Shop of the Year' award, a most deserved accolade for this forward going business.

Prize-winning sheep remain an important facet of Dales life, providing us all with food and a connection with the landscape that is much in need of celebration and understanding.

Farmers Markets

Farmers markets are the perfect opportunity to buy all your fresh local produce at one time. The stallholders genuinely enjoy meeting with the food buying public. It gives them an opportunity to understand what people are looking for in a product and also to explain the process of getting it from the field to the plate.

It is often suggested that markets should be held more frequently than once a month to enable people to have good access to fresh local produce on a regular basis. However, this can be impractical for the market stallholders, as it should be remembered that for the majority their first priority is to farm, and this in itself is a full time role.

Northern Dales Farmers Markets is a social enterprise company, which means that any profits are re-invested for the benefit of the group. It was established in 2000 when eighteen farmers held the first market in Richmond. Under the leadership of Alastair Davy, a hill farmer from the Richmond area, the markets have flourished and there are now ten each month, spread from Darlington in the north to Skipton in the south.

All the Northern Dales Farmers Markets are accredited by the national Farmers Retail and Markets Association. To gain accreditation they must conform to quite stringent guidelines. As well as the expected Health and Safety and food hygiene regulations, the rules also state that the person selling the produce must have been directly involved in its growing, harvesting or preparation. This is great for consumers, as you know the person who is serving you is entirely familiar with the products. In the case of processed goods, such as pies or cakes, a high percentage of the ingredients should be sourced locally. A meat pie cannot be made with imported beef and ideally the pastry will have used local flour and butter.

The stallholders form their own community and buy from each other. In the northern Dales, Alastair co-ordinates a regular delivery of produce from the stallholders to local schools in the Richmond area. This keeps him busy during the week as

Northern Dales Farmers Markets is run to precision by Alastair Davy, who here takes a rare break from early morning driving and organisation to help set up a local food festival.

(Left) Come rain or shine the stalls at Settle farmers market are there laden with local goodies and brilliant banter. There is no better way of getting fresh - sometimes picked that morning – local produce.

(Right) Grassington farmers market provides an opportunity to meet up with friends, share recipes and ideas, support your local farmers and take home bags of fresh healthy food.

most of the markets are held at the weekend. It is hoped in the future to expand this area of operation as it offers the stallholders enhanced benefits. The schools and other public sector outlets often require cheaper cuts of meat such as mince and stewing steak. Our children can benefit from high-quality products that can be traced back to the farm and the farmers can then consider selling their higher-value cuts, such as fillet and sirloin, to the restaurant trade – all of which makes perfect sense but does take a high degree of co-ordination.

Within the Dales, and on the Trails, you can visit most of the markets in the group. The first market of the month is Stokesley, some distance from the Dales Trails but handy for visitors travelling to the area from the North East. It takes place in the square and usually features over twenty-five stallholders.

The first market on our Trails is Skipton, held on the first Sunday in the month, in a beautiful canalside setting, just off Coach Street. There is on-site parking and the stalls are set out in a pedestrianised area giving an almost continental feel. Skipton is handy for the Wharfedale, Malhamdale and Ribblesdale Trails.

One week later, on the second Sunday of the month the market is at Settle, which is at the heart of the Ribblesdale Trail. Parking here is close-by and the stalls cover two sides of the Market Place in the shadow of Castlebergh and alongside the imposing buildings that make up the Shambles.

Richmond Farmers Market takes place on the third Saturday of the month in the Market Place. There is parking nearby and a superb variety of shops stocking locally produced goods are also open throughout the day. Richmond is on the Swaledale Trail.

On the third Sunday of the month you are spoilt for choice, as there are markets in both Grassington and Ripon. That at Grassington – on the Wharfedale Trail – takes place in the cobbled square and you can park within a short, level walk at the National Park Centre. The venue at Ripon, handy for the Nidderdale Trail, is the central Market Place close to free disc parking.

The final Saturday of the month is Leyburn Market, again held in the Market Place. As at Richmond, the shops are open too so you can make a day of it. Leyburn is featured on our Wensleydale Trail.

In addition to those mentioned above, Northern Dales Farmers Markets also run markets in Northallerton on the fourth Wednesday of the month, Hartlepool on the second Saturday and at Nature's World, Acklam, near Middlesbrough, on the last Sunday.

For many farmers, growers and food producers the markets have provided a whole new way of life. When once they would have waved goodbye to their livestock at the farm gate and sent them off to an unknown buyer, probably for them to end up on the shelves of a supermarket in anonymous packaging, now they go through the whole process. The difference in returns is also significant. Selling through a market to a large buyer returns low profits. By selling direct or through small independent retailers they are cutting out so many 'middle men' that they can actually begin to see a bright future for their businesses again.

Many of our featured producers can be seen at the farmers markets. However, with up to twenty-five stallholders, including some based outside our Trail areas, there are so many others who deserve a mention:

Stamfrey Farm Clotted Cream

Sue Gaudie is of Cornish origin; she married Angus, a Yorkshireman and moved to West Rounton near Northallerton. Together they farm over 250 acres and in

Hard work and planning during the year means Katrina from Bluebell Organic Farm can offer fresh, healthy, nutrient-packed produce – picked, pickled or pressed – even in the depth of winter.

recent years have converted their dairy herd to organic. Of all the things Sue missed about her former life, clotted cream had to be one of the most significant. Her friends were asked to bring cream on their visits north and eventually one arrived with a separator, the piece of equipment required to make clotted cream. Now available in farm shops around the county, Stamfrey Farm Clotted Cream has recently been joined on the shelves by yoghurt. This ensures the very best use is made of all the organic milk produced at Stamfrey Farm. Despite selling into such prestigious outlets as Betty's, the wonderful group of Yorkshire tea rooms, Sue still enjoys her monthly trip to Northallerton Farmers Market where she catches up with her customers old and new.

Bluebell Organics

Katrina Palmer created Bluebell Organics (Swaledale Trail map – 6) when she moved to Forcett near Richmond in

RECIPE: Carrot and Celeriac Layers

From Stephanie Moon, Executive Chef of Rudding Park Hotel, this dish using freshly picked produce from one of the Northern Dales Farmers Markets is ideal for a dinner party. It looks incredibly impressive, tastes delicious and is best made the day before, as it easier to stamp out the layers when cold and it also avoids that last minute panic! It can be served as an accompaniment to any meat dish, or alone with a green salad as a vegetarian dish.

4 large peeled thinly sliced carrots sliced long ways
1 head of celeriac, peeled and thinly sliced
1 pint of double cream,
3 pieces crushed garlic
salt and pepper
1 small bunch of thyme - pick the leaves and discard the stalks

Layer the celeriac and carrot in an ovenproof greased dish. Bring the double cream to the boil with the crushed garlic, then remove the garlic and discard. Pouring the seasoned cream over each layer. Sprinkle over the thyme leaves. Bake at 180 degrees/Gas mark 5 for about half an hour until cooked through. When cooked, stamp out in metal rings and serve. If made the previous day, re-heat for around 15 minutes in a hot oven prior to serving.

2000 to begin work on a previously derelict walled garden. In 2001 her partner Steve Barker joined her and together they have worked hard to build up the company through farmers markets and a home-delivery scheme. At the garden they grow a wide range of protected crops like salad, tomatoes, peppers and cucumbers and there is a large apple orchard and several other fruit trees. Working in partnership with others locally, they are also able to grow larger quantities of bulkier crops such as potatoes, carrots and onions. You can see Katrina on Richmond Farmers Market, or if you live locally, enjoy a regular weekly box delivered to your door.

Bracken Hill Fine Foods

After twenty years making preserves for other people Neil decided to go it alone and, with the support of his wife Gill, Bracken Hill Fine Foods was born. Neil produces marmalades, jams, curds, chutneys, jellies, sauces and mustards to complement and enhance many types of food. During 2004, their first year of operation, they gained no less than nine 'Great Taste Awards' from the Guild of Fine Food Retailers. Neil makes all his recipes the traditional way in small batches using open pans and does not add any artificial preservatives or colouring. Both Neil and Gill began life in agriculture and it is important to them both to use the best ingredients from local growers where possible. You will find Bracken Hill in many of the retail outlets detailed here and also at all of the farmers markets that we feature.

Scarcliffe Farm Yorkshire Lamb

When we initially met Ross Greenwood he had to go out to work as a builder three days a week to supplement the income he was able to derive from rearing and selling traditional breed lamb and beef. Ross had just taken the plunge and booked a stall at the first farmers market to be held in Skipton. He now does five markets a month, has given up the day job and in between the markets has a successful business delivering beef and lamb to his customers. Based at Carleton near Skipton he lives with his parents on their farm, which is part of the Broughton Hall estate. See Ross at Skipton, Grassington and Settle markets.

CONTACT DETAILS

Stamfrey Farm Clotted Cream, *Stamfrey Farm, West Rounton, Northallerton, DL6 2AJ (not open to visitors)* T 01609 882297

Bracken Hill Fine Foods, *7 Cranbrooks Close, Wheldrake, York, YO19 6BY (not open to visitors)* T 01904 448286 www.brackenhillfinefoods.co.uk

Scarcliffe Farm Yorkshire Lamb, *Scarcliffe Farm, Carleton, Skipton, BD23 3HS (not open to visitors)* T 077250 45572

Shows and Festivals

Agricultural shows have been a part of the rural calendar for as long as there have been sheep on the hills, and at least one features on most of the Trails. We hope you will enjoy visiting the shows and supporting the local producers. Such events are an opportunity for the whole community to come together to catch up with neighbours and with friends from out of the area. Produce ranging from cattle to the best fruit cake is presented with a pride so often lacking in modern-day life.

In recent years the three shows that take place in Craven – Gargrave, Malham and Kilnsey – have created a specific area to host Northern Dales Farmers Markets and other local producers. At other shows there is often a variety of trade stalls, usually made up of produce from the area. The main shows in the Dales calendar are:

Gargrave – second to last Saturday in August
Malham – last Saturday in August
Upper Wharfedale (Kilnsey) – August Bank Holiday Tuesday
Wensleydale (Leyburn) – last Saturday in August
Swaledale (Reeth) – last Wednesday in August
Nidderdale (Pateley Bridge) – last Monday in September

In addition to the agricultural shows some of the areas have developed their own speciality food festivals. Leyburn Festival of Food and Drink was the first of these and is now well established in the Dales calendar. It takes place on the May Day Bank Holiday weekend and is a three-day event held on the showfield on the outskirts of the town. There are well over a hundred exhibitors, along with both food and farming demonstrations. A recent show included such delights in the cookery theatre as:

Anne Shedden – from Ladies in Pigs

A wonderful organisation with one very clear objective – to increase the consumption of British pork and bacon by demonstrating the versatility of different cuts, and remind consumers of the quality of pork produced in the UK.

Canons Brian Abell and Lesley Morley

The 'Cooking Canons', representing the Royal Agricultural Benevolent Institution. This is a national charity dedicated to helping members of the farming community facing hardship.

The Wensleydale Creamery

Watch the expert cheese maker turn milk from the dale into a real Wensleydale Cheese during a short demonstration, replicating how they traditionally undertake the process at the Wensleydale Creamery in Hawes.

Skipton Festival of Food and Drink is now in its third year. Initiated by North Yorkshire County Council in 2003, it was then taken on by Feast. We re-named the event Autumn Feast to tie in with our seasonal produce ethos and moved the venue from the Auction Mart on the outskirts of town to the grounds of Skipton Castle for year two. However, having outgrown this venue, it will now move back to the Auction Mart for its third year.

Autumn Feast comprises a cookery theatre, where we feature a celebrity chef, often one of the BBC's 'Ready Steady Cook' team, alongside top local chefs. The common theme throughout is cooking with local produce. Autumn Feast coincides with the National British Food Fortnight.

Customer care is a family affair for Steven Crabtree from Bolton Abbey Foods, with his wife Ann and daughter Beth 'womaning' the stall at the Autumn Feast Food Festival at Skipton.

Producers exhibit and sell at the show and this gives us an opportunity to introduce a few who fall just outside the area of the trails but who are none the less important to the local food scene:

Steenbergs – Organic Herbs and Spices

Sophie and Axel Steenberg launched their range of organic spices in February 2004 and the organic loose leaf tea in January 2005. They felt that the quality and variety of herbs and spices generally available wasn't what they sought, and they also wanted much greater provenance and traceability.

Steenbergs is an organic spices and tea business and ethically buys all its products. Sophie and Axel worked hard with producers to be the first company in the UK to offer spices carrying the 'Fairtrade' mark. They buy many of their spices and herbs direct from producers – to ensure greater freshness and provenance. All the blends are their own and are created in a small factory on the edge of the Dales. More recently they have launched a range of premium organic loose leaf tea, available in aluminium canisters and kraft bags, four or which carry the 'Fairtrade' mark. This came about because of the synergy between spice producers and tea – most pepper is grown as a shade tree within a coffee or tea plantation. So although spices and tea do not grow in the Dales this is a fine example of how you can make sure you are fairly supporting local traders throughout the world.

Steenbergs products can be found in many of the outlets mentioned on our Trails including Sticky Ginger at Askrigg, the Wine Cave (part of the Angel at Hetton), Kilnsey Trout Farm and at some local shows.

Swillington Organic Farm

Sited on the outskirts of Leeds, Swillington Farm is a haven of peace and tranquillity unlike any place I have ever previously encountered. It is a cross between secret garden and animal farm. Housed in the walled garden of a country house, with relics of statues strewn around the place, it boasts an array of organic fruit and vegetables. Just beyond the walls of the garden are acres and acres of green fields full of happy rare breed pigs, native breed cattle and sheep.

Jo Cartwright is the one-woman powerhouse behind the whole enterprise, working from pre dawn to post dusk, assisted by family members and friends. Jo has developed an organic farm, her own butchery department and a farm shop as well as finding time to visit local shows and farmers markets on a regular basis.

Tribute to the pie makers

We haven't featured too many pie makers in this book, which is strange as there are so many good ones in the area. Skipton is famous for Stanforths Pork Pies, bought from the tiny butchers shop on Mill Bridge, just by the canal. Stanforths also supply the pies to many catering and retail outlets throughout the Dales.

Drake and Macefield with shops in both Skipton and Settle, have won many awards over the years. (see page 48).

On many of the farmers markets in the region you will see Rose Cottage Foods. Rupert originally produced all the meat on their own farm but, due to demand, now buys a lot from friends who are in farming. Their extensive range is well known throughout the region and includes pork & blue cheese pie, sausage & tomato pie, and chicken & ham pie. Other favourites include Huntsman's Pie, which is layers of pork and chicken topped with sage & onion stuffing, and the Butler's Pie - a layer of pork, cranberry sauce and a layer of turkey, which is perfect at Christmas time. Rose Cottage are usually one of the first stalls to sell out at the shows they attend in the Dales.

Thornhill Dexter Beef

Another woman on a mission is Penny Hodgson, who from her farm in the Vale of York rears Dexter Beef to the very highest of standards. The first Dexters in Penny's life were bought as companions for a Shetland 'house' cow, which she had purchased with the idea of producing beef and milk. She wanted to feed her children with products from animals that had been fed and reared naturally. Penny soon became very fond of this small breed of cattle, and started increasing the herd. Sadly, she lost her first herd in the Foot and Mouth epidemic, so decided to move to Thornhill Farm in Easingwold to try to escape the bad memories. Once there, with the beginnings of a new herd,

RECIPE: Quick Cheesy Leeks

Serves 4. Sally created this one chilly October afternoon in the run-up to Autumn Feast. Everything goes on hold – our families' wonder who we are and get used to fending for themselves for at least a week before the event. Having returned from setting up one afternoon, Sally found the cupboards were bare. Gathering what she could muster from the dwindling pantry she put this dish together and it was lovely!

3 medium leeks
55g (2oz) butter
110g (4oz) Swaledale cheese
1 brown or white bloomer
Salt & pepper

Roughly chop the leeks and fry in half the butter. Slice the bloomer in the half-inch slices and butter. Place in an ovenproof dish. Spoon over the leeks and cover with grated cheese. Bake in a hot oven for about 10 minutes until the cheese has melted.

Penny decided to establish whether there was a market for the beef by putting a sign out at the end of the farm drive. The response was excellent and once customers had tried the taste of Dexter beef they came back for more and also recommended it to other people.

The motto of the farm is 'Pampered cows, Perfect beef'. Penny believes in giving her herd a happy, natural environment with mothers deciding when to wean their calves and keeping family groups and friends together. The herd has expanded significantly in the past four years, so that it is now one of the largest in the North of England. The beef business has expanded too, and is gaining an excellent reputation. Many customers still purchase it from the farm, but it also available by mail order and from delicatessens and farm shops. Thornhill Dexter Beef features in Rick Stein's 'Guide to Food Heroes of Britain' and Antony Worrall Thompson has recently described it as "excellent". Penny's final word though: "Regardless of its success, one of the most important things is that at the end of a day there is enough time to sit on a bale of hay and watch the calves play."

71

Dawn and Lisa

To conclude on a sweet note we just have to mention two of our absolute favourites, Dawn Carvey and Lisa Hodgson – whose respective businesses are aptly named 'Traditional and Scrumptious' and Loopy Lisa's

From her farmhouse kitchen on the borders of County Durham, Dawn prepares a wonderful selection of home baking, from oozy lemon drizzle cakes to seasonal fruit delights, Stollen at Christmas, Simnel for Easter and a regular selection of fruity treats to grace the finest of tea trays.

Lisa is the 'Fudge Queen of the North'. This is fudge like it should be – sugary, melty, sweet beyond your wildest dreams but above all real! Until I tried this at Autumn Feast 2005 I had given up hope. The fudge I remembered as a child had gone – or so I thought. Lisa thought so too and decided the only way she would get the real fudge for which she craved was to make it herself. So she did – and still does! It is available at shows throughout the Dales and in many of the retail outlets mentioned on the Trails. If you buy nothing else in some shops you simply can't pass this by!

CONTACT DETAILS

Steenbergs - Organic Herbs and Spices, *PO Box 48, Boroughbridge, York, YO51 9ZW (not open to visitors)* ✆ 01765 640088 ⓘ www.steenbergs.co.uk

Swillington Organic Farm, *Coach Road, Swillington, Leeds, LS26 8QA* ✆ 0113 2869129 ⓘ www.swillingtonorganicfarm.co.uk

Drake and Macefield, *Independent Family Butchers, 11 Otley Street, Skipton* ✆ 01756 792802 ⓘ skipton@drakeandmacefield.co.uk (Also at: Market Place, Settle T 01729 822392 E settle@drakeandmacefield.co.uk) www.drakeandmacefield.co.uk

Rose Cottage Foods, *Unit 17 Kellythorpe Industrial Estate, Driffield, YO25 9DJ* ✆ 01377 257700 ⓘ www.rose-cottage-foods.com

Thornhill Dexter Beef, *Thornhill Farm, Thirsk Road, Easingwold, YO61 3ND (not open to visitors)* ✆ 01347 823827

Traditional and Scrumptious, *Cockleberry House, West Lane, Dalton-on-Tees, DL2 2PP (not open to visitors)* ✆ 01325 378053 ⓘ www.traditionalandscrumptious.co.uk

Loopy Lisa's Fudge, *4 Loop Lane, Butterknowle, Bishop Auckland, DL13 5JR (not open to visitors)* ✆ 01388 718794

GENERAL INFORMATION

Nidderdale ⓘ www.nidderdale.co.uk ✆ 0845 3890 179

Wharfedale Tourist Information ⓘ www.skipton-web.co.uk ✆ 01756 792809

Malhamdale ⓘ www.malhamdale.com ✆ 01729 830 363

Ribblesdale ⓘ www.settle.org.uk ✆ 01729 825192

Wensleydale ⓘ www.wensleydale.net Tourist Information: ⓘ www.leyburn.yorkshiredales.net ✆ 01969 623069

Swaledale Tourist Information: ⓘ www.richmond.org.uk ✆ 01748 850252

Yorkshire Dales National Park Authority ⓘ www.yorkshiredales.org.uk ✆ 08701 666 333

Yorkshire Dales Tourism Partnership ⓘ www.yorkshiredales.org ✆ 01729 825 470

For details on the Farmers Markets ⓘ www.ndfms.co.uk ✆ 01756 748 627